Jessica McClintock's

SIMPLY

Romantic

DECORATING

Jessica McClintock's

SIMPLY

Romantic

DECORATING

Creating Elegance and Intimacy
Throughout Your Home

JESSICA McCLINTOCK
with Karen Kelly

Rodale books may be purchased for business or promotional use or for special sales.
For information, please write to: Special Markets Department, Rodale Inc.,
733 Third Avenue, New York, NY 10017

Printed in the United States of America
Rodale Inc. makes every effort to use acid-free ♾, recycled paper ♻.

All photos by Rory Earnshaw, with the exception of the following:
pages 58, 61, and 65: Courtesy of C.R. Laine
page 72: Courtesy of American Drew
page 115: Courtesy of Lea Industries, Inc.

Book design by SPELL, New York

Library of Congress Cataloging-in-Publication Data

McClintock, Jessica.
Jessica McClintock's simply romantic decorating : creating elegance and
intimacy throughout your home / Jessica McClintock with Karen Kelly.
p. cm.
ISBN-13 978–1–59486–467–4 hardcover
ISBN-10 1–59486–467–5 hardcover
1. Interior decoration—Psychological aspects. I. Title. II. Title:
Simply romantic decorating.
NK2113.M23 2006
747—dc222006028988

Distributed to the trade by Holtzbrinck Publishers

2   4   6   8   10   9   7   5   3   1   hardcover

We inspire and enable people to improve their lives and the world around them
For more of our products visit **rodalestore.com** or call 800-848-4735

Contents

Foreword by Chris Madden vii

Part One

SETTING THE STAGE FOR ROMANTIC STYLE
CHAPTER ONE: Inspiration and Philosophy 2
CHAPTER TWO: Beautiful Backgrounds 22

Part Two

DESIGNED FOR ROMANTIC LIVING
CHAPTER THREE: The Social Home: Living Rooms 52
CHAPTER FOUR: Cooking, Dining, and Entertaining 78
CHAPTER FIVE: Private Moments: Bedrooms and Bathrooms 106
CHAPTER SIX: In-Between Spaces and Hidden Rooms 132
CHAPTER SEVEN: Nature Perfected: Garden Rooms and Gardens 144

Part Three

ROMANTIC PROJECTS
CHAPTER EIGHT: Beautiful Background Projects 162
CHAPTER NINE: Soft Furnishings 174
CHAPTER TEN: Decorative Accessories and Painted Furniture 188

Stencil Templates 206
Resources 210
Acknowledgments 211
Index 212

FOREWORD

The sweet summers of the south of France, the elegant steps of Fred and Ginger, the cinematic sensuousness of *Doctor Zhivago*, a cool rendition of a Cole Porter song—each evokes for me the style and aesthetic of my friend Jessica McClintock. Her finely tuned vision creates design we all instantly recognize . . . her romantic prom dresses, chic evening gowns, an elegant settee, a garden-like fragrance, and lace, lace, and more lace—each defining the inimitable style of Jessica.

I've had the privilege and pleasure of televising and photographing Jessica's home for many of my books, and I've enjoyed a serene cup of tea with her (and her dogs!) at the end of our workday in her home's romantic ambience, which is her acknowledged universal signature.

What a treat now to have *Simply Romantic Decorating* and this wonderful opportunity to have access to and absorb firsthand Jessica's roadmap to creating her take on the romantic style in your own home. And, as you might expect, she does so in her own unique fashion—with personal anecdotes, worldly advice, and classical references from which she draws her own inspirations—literature, music, architecture, and art.

From her 18th-century French kitchen and indoor garden room, to her Victorian-era bathroom and breathtakingly beautiful bedroom—I find myself drawn to these special places again and again. These rooms inspire me, and in them, I always discover a delicious new layer on which to focus. Even when I'm on the road traveling throughout America lecturing and speaking with women about helping them to define their own personal styles and turn their homes into their havens, I love to share my photographs of Jessica's spaces. These images are met with great enthusiasm, and what follows is usually an intense interest and discussion in all of the details of her rooms. People seem to discover a sense of connection (whether it relates to their own lives or not) in these wonderfully romantic settings.

In *Simply Romantic Decorating*, Jessica reveals the magic of her design style and shows us how to create rooms that are warm, embracing, sensually stimulating, personally rich, and, occasionally, quietly intimate. She imbues this handsome book with a sense of living in the moment and illustrates how our surroundings can add layers of richness to our daily lives. She invites you into her most intimate interior spaces and—through her lush descriptions, practical "know-how" advice, and instructions—shows you how to achieve this wonderfully romantic ambience. It's pure Jessica—and I know you'll enjoy this journey as much as I did.

CHRIS MADDEN
interior designer and author
of *A Room of Her Own*

Part One
SETTING THE STAGE FOR ROMANTIC STYLE

A lacy gown, a stolen kiss, the pop of a champagne cork. Romance is simple, sublime, and celebratory. It transcends the everyday and moves beyond the mass-produced. Indeed, the Romantic movement treasured boundless imagination, individualism, sentimentalism, natural beauty, the picturesque past, remote places, and antiquity. What wonderful ideas. All of them are captured in my vision of romantic design, which is Old World, soft, and subtle. It's a blend of muted colors, curved and feminine lines, beautifully proportioned arrangements, and dramatic architecture.

Yes, I have definite opinions about romantic style, but your home and the way you decorate it is very personal. Find things you like and then follow my guidelines to find your own definition of romance. The best way to begin is to get into a romantic mood by exploring literature, art, and nature. Learn from the past. And don't forget to dream. Let your thoughts run free—put no limits on them. All of my great creative endeavors started with inspiration and imagination. That's how new and exciting design ideas are born.

I have been a fashion designer for many years, and no matter what the trends, I have always stayed with classic silhouettes and feminine fabrics like lace, satin, and velvet. I make the kind of clothes that women are drawn to no matter what's being shown in the fashion magazines of the moment. A cream-colored lace blouse or a black velvet skirt is always in style. The blouse, paired with the latest jeans, looks modern. The skirt is so basic and lovely that it serves as an anchor for a trendy top or jacket.

I feel the same about home design. Classic styles, beautifully made, stand the test of time and can be accessorized to fit changing tastes. I love a home that offers a soft and cuddling feeling, a refuge from the world, where I feel protected and comfortable. Timeless, not trendy, romantic style transcends fads and fashions and, as a result, always looks beautiful, never dated. Its reliance on classic ideas about proportion and line lets you bring history into your home through color, furnishings, fabrics, and accessories without having to slavishly reproduce an 18th-century English drawing room or copy a 17th-century French boudoir down to the last detail. The subtle, monochromatic palette means you can be inspired by many styles rooted in the past and blend them for a completely fresh but still harmonious combination of furnishings, textiles, and finishes.

Romantic decorating is not "don't touch" design—it's very livable, very inviting. It is more than just a certain piece of furniture or a color palette. Yes, those elements are important to a romantic setting. But you live in a home—you sleep, eat, read, relax, and share wonderful times with friends and family in your home. Our daily lives should never be constrained because the chairs are too fancy for sitting or the rug is too rare for the dogs to curl up on. Romantic style replenishes your energy, keeps you grounded, and transports you to another world without making you feel like a guest in your own house. Surround yourself with beauty and softness and you feel special. Any space can become a beautifully worked jewel box. It begins by understanding the classic principles of romantic design and getting the wall color and background details just right. Some daydreaming is required, too. You can't have romance without a little fantasy.

Chapter One

INSPIRATION AND PHILOSOPHY

Romantic inspiration is everywhere—if you know how and where to look. I have always found mine in books, music, art, movies, nature, my own imagination, and life experiences. I guess I have a romantic soul—and if you are reading this book, you probably have one as well. We can easily get out of the habit of using our imaginations, because we are so busy, and it's hard to make the effort to see what is all around us or to seek out beauty in museums, walks in the park, and historical areas of our own neighborhoods. Romantic living means paying attention to, appreciating, and enjoying our surroundings. You get so much back from it.

When daydreaming is part of your mind-set, romance comes naturally. I have had a lifetime to develop my imagination, starting with my country childhood in rural Maine. I am so lucky that I am able to focus it on what I love—fashion and interior design. I was alone a lot as a young girl because my older sister was much more social than I was, and she was always out and about. There was no television to pass the time. Instead, I spent a lot of time reading, and my favorites were books about young girls in romantic situations, such as *Anne of Green Gables, Wuthering Heights,* and *Pride and Prejudice.* I would picture myself on the moors, riding a horse and wearing a long skirt with ruffles and cowboy boots, the grass sweeping the ends of my skirt and my ankles. It was very exciting, even if it was only in my mind.

In college, I continued my studies with enthusiasm, and I enjoyed reading about everything—art, history, even science. I married an MIT man—he was a businessman, but metallurgy was

his specialty. All of his friends were intellectuals and scientists, but I never repressed my romantic point of view for their benefit—they liked it. It softened them. So the beauty of romantic decorating appeals to men and women, especially if you keep it symmetrical, soothing, and welcoming (qualities men seem to love).

My first husband died when he was only thirty-four, and afterward a good friend gave me *The Little Prince,* by Antoine de Saint-Exupéry. If you don't know the story, it is about a pilot who crashes in the Sahara Desert and meets a boy, the little prince, from another planet, and together they

> In style, the Romantics favored luxury and lushness to the preceding neoclassical age's preference for restraint.

it was so beautifully photographed. If you have a romantic soul, you will love it. The details, everything about the way the characters moved and talked, and the action between the families are very different from the way I grew up. It was mysterious and secretive, like a faded dream, and that enveloped me. Anything that transports you out of yourself and the everyday world is romantic. The new version of *Pride and Prejudice* is so fantastic. *The New World* is also so lovely and moving and beautifully photographed. Let the set design, color palette, or historical period of beautiful romantic films inspire your own decorating ideas. The exotic set of *Memoirs of a Geisha* might prompt you to add Japanese vases and textiles to your living room. The natural palette of *The New World* may lead you to paint your walls a soft, mossy green. See how easy it is to get carried away by ninety minutes of celluloid dreams?

I design dresses and fashion accessories as well as home furnishings, so I am curious about what

is going on in the fashion world. Fashion has always inspired my home designs. There is a connection between what I do with fashion design and what I do with home and furniture design. I always have stacks of fashion magazines around my house, so I can flip through them anytime to see what's new or revisit past ideas. Fashion and home textiles are fun to look at and examine. A print on a dressmaker's fabric may suggest an idea for a drapery. The ruffle on a dress might be translated into a ruffle on a pillow. Woven brocades or ethnic block prints could send me in a whole other direction. Something as deceptively simple as the color of a sun-faded velvet jacket may inspire a color story or a design scheme of a room. A slightly dusty, old pink velvet rose spotted on a ladies' hat at a secondhand shop might prompt you to do over your boudoir in cream-tinged rose and dove gray. Even my favorite model, Heather, is a source of inspiration—I consider her my muse!

Fine art, of course, feeds the romantic soul. Even though I don't hang art on my walls (I prefer to let the architectural features of my home, such as doors, windows, and moldings, take on the role of "art"), I am still captivated by 18th- and 19th-century landscapes and portraits. They show us a dreamy world—magical moments lost to time but alive in our imaginations. Walk through a museum and let all the imagery wash over you. Does what you see initiate a color scheme? The work of bolder artists like Gauguin and Matisse or modern masters such as Jackson Pollack and Picasso (some of my favorites) are so educational. I would not use their bold palettes in my home, but their paintings teach me a great deal about the relationships among color, shape, and line.

✳ ABOVE: *The evening gowns I design inspire my ideas about home décor.*

✳ OPPOSITE: *Fashion and design converge in my life. Note how the rouching on the dress that I am fitting on Heather is similar to the detail on my window treatments.*

Architecture stimulates ideas. Great castles and chateaus of Europe are, of course, a source of many of my ideas. Versailles, with its richly carved and painted architectural details, even on the smallest doorknob or narrow piece of trim, and the soft colors used throughout the interior, is a feast for the eyes and the mind. My favorite book on the subject is *Unseen Versailles*, by the legendary photographer Deborah Turbeville. She captures the hidden spaces of this enchanted place, and I find it extremely stirring and exciting.

Yet you don't have to travel to another continent for insight. The gentle curve of an arched window on a house in your own neighborhood may motivate you to add oval picture-frame moldings to the walls of your living room. You just have to open your eyes and look around. My own home inspires me—it was built in 1889, well before the famous Golden Gate Bridge was erected in 1937 and just seventeen years before the earthquake of 1906. (My house stood firm during that devastating catastrophe.) An early photograph taken a few years after the house was built shows a dirt road and no other buildings around it. Today, it is surrounded by Italianate-, French-, and Victorian-style houses. San Francisco is a romantic city—its undulating streets and hilly terrain are very Old World. I cannot imagine a modern city being built on a hill like this was.

Nature is instructive when it comes to color, symmetry, and harmony. It is perfectly designed, down to the tiniest ladybug or blade of grass. Slow down the next time you are out for a walk. Look past the obvious and toward the unique details that are hidden at first glance. Trellis roses or ivy noticed while on a stroll through a garden can spark a desire to paint a pale vine of flowers on your walls. Indulge an idea sparked by nature—or art or anything. That's how professional designers get ideas for room and color schemes.

Why, even my three Labrador retrievers inspire me—Coco Chanel and the twins, Rose and Lily. Their black and cream silken hair is glamorous,

✳ ABOVE: *The history of my 1889 Victorian home is a constant source of romantic design ideas.*

✳ OPPOSITE, TOP: *Old family photos from days gone by (that's me with the little bob haircut) are a romantic reminder of simpler, gentler times.*

✳ OPPOSITE, BOTTOM: *Old books transport you to other times and places.*

their soft brown eyes are so friendly, and their unconditional love is a miracle. They remind me of how elegant a bit of black added to an eggshell palette looks. It may seem odd for a pet to inspire a decorating scheme, but it demonstrates a way of thinking, of always keeping your eyes open to possibility.

✳ ABOVE: *Surrounding yourself with the beauty of nature is a helpful and beautiful way to get new ideas about color schemes. Some roses from the garden, arranged in a simple glass vase lined with a leaf and placed on my mantel, might inspire me to create an entire collection of dresses in various shades of pink—or motivate me to change the fabrics in my living room from cream to rose.*

✳ LEFT: *One of my three precious Labradors, Rose. Their total and unconditional love and devotion cannot help but inspire me.*

CREATE A DESIGN JOURNAL

Sometimes a piece of fabric or a pretty flower is enough to get me started on a new design idea. A good way to keep track of all the ideas and images that strike you is with a design journal. A plain-paper journal from a stationery or office-supply store, covered with a favorite fabric or scrap of wallpaper (in your color palette, of course) is the perfect place to store and keep track of fabric swatches, paint chips, and pictures from design magazines or art books. Take it with you when you shop so you can take notes on stores you like, model numbers of furnishings, or any thoughts and ideas that strike a romantic chord. When you are ready to decorate, the journal will come in handy as a reference. A design journal is a wonderful resource if you are also using a professional designer—he or she can draw from it to get a clear picture of what you like and how you think.

✳ ABOVE: *Fabric swatches are handy and convenient reminders of color schemes. I collect swatches from fabrics in each room of my house and keep them with me whenever I am shopping for accessories so I know my purchases will blend in with what I already have in the room.*

The French and Italian styles of the 17th and 18th centuries have definitely shaped my ideas about interior design. Many visitors to my home say it's Louis Seize—that's the Louis period of decoration that prevailed in France between 1774 and 1793—it is characterized by simple opulence, gently curved lines, symmetry, and slender, feminine proportion. Colors were generally light or pale in tone, sometimes with a touch of gilding; ornament was rich yet delicate and in low relief, embossed, or painted. Slender fluted legs, convex moldings, and rosette, leaf,

and flower motifs were often found in furniture and architectural details. Upholstery, drapes, and table coverings were made from silks and velvets in a variety of textures and finishes. Those elements are echoed throughout my home—but Louis style is not the only interpretation of romantic style. I also love 18th- and 19th-century English and Italian furnishings and textiles. My garden courtyard, designed by Willis Polk, for example, is very much inspired by Italian design.

This glimpse at romantic interior design styles may move you to read about the history of decorating and inspire your own design schemes.

BAROQUE: *Exaggerated and exuberant lines and dramatic and bold curving forms, along with elaborate ornamentation characterize this movement. Highly decorative motifs found on furniture and walls were boldly and deeply carved and included mythological animals, lush garlands of fruit and flowers, and the fleur-de-lis. The style started around 1600 in Rome, Italy, and spread to most of Europe, lasting until 1715. Caravaggio was the most important baroque painter.*

ROCOCO: *The term itself comes from the French word rocaille, which means "rock work." Playful, pretty, whimsical, and soft lines and colors characterize the style, first popular from about 1715 to 1775, especially in France and Germany. It favors small-scale furnishings and ornate decoration, pastels, and the asymmetrical, but perfectly balanced, arrangement of curves and other forms.*

LOUIS SEIZE: *Simple but soft, slender lines in perfect proportion were emphasized in furniture. Colors were light, and pastels and muted color were preferred in finishes and textiles; ornaments and carvings were delicate and in low relief, embossed, painted, or gilded. Slender fluted legs and intricate carving defined furniture. Flower and leaf motifs found on carved frames and molding were often painted white and touched with gilt. Upholstery and draperies used varied fabrics such as velvet, satin, silk, and taffeta.*

GOTHIC REVIVAL: *This style movement started in the mid-18th century in England and lasted well into the 19th century in Europe and North America. It sought to revive medieval forms, in contrast to more rigidly defined classical styles (think straight lines) that were popular. It was characterized by slender and soaring curved lines, flying buttresses, pointed arches, and rib-vaulted ceilings. Detailed carving was found on furniture. Dark wood was prominent, but today gothic pieces can be lightened with some pastel paint or with a process that creates a bleached wood effect.*

ART NOUVEAU: *Dynamic, undulating, and flowing curved lines characterize the designs of this popular early 20th-century movement. Much of the inspiration for Art Nouveau can be found in the plant world. Even though it was thought to be modern at the time, aficionados looked back to the abstract elements of rococo style, such as shell motifs, and simplified them to suit a more modern idea. Highly stylized interpretations of seaweed,* grasses, flowers, and even insects found their way onto picture and mirror frames, furniture, and textiles.

ART DECO: *This modern style began in France and was popular in much of Europe and the United States from about 1915 to 1925. Even though sharp geometric lines and chrome characterize some art deco design, it has a lot of romantic features: Mirrored furniture, satin and silk upholstery, sophisticated pastel tones, and sleek curves are very glamorous, sexy, and elegant.*

The Language of Romantic Decorating

No matter where you find your romance, there are certain principles that help you keep focused.

Sophistication

Romantic decorating doesn't have to be excessively sweet and naïve. Many people may initially hear the word *romantic* and assume it means lots of pink ruffles, hearts, overblown cabbage roses, and scented candles. Those elements can certainly be part of the language of romance. The more refined version I am partial to is classical and subdued. It takes time to find special pieces like American antiques and those imported from abroad or to seek out unique, carefully crafted, or one-of-a-kind objects and furnishings. Sophistication is having the mind-set, "If I can't find what I want, I will have it made or make it myself . . . or wait until it comes along." Don't settle for anything less than beautiful.

Luxury

The conventional definition of luxury is "something that is self-indulgent and not necessary." I could not disagree more. Luxury is essential, especially in the romantic home. It's an attitude as much as it is an object or a quality. It is a wonderful bouquet of flowers, creamy bars of French milled soap, a stack of thick and fluffy white towels in the bathroom, a bowl of dew-kissed raspberries on the breakfast table, a recording of an Italian opera or a string quartet playing the background for dinner or while you get ready for the day; it's a long frothy bubble bath or a glass of good wine. Luxury is a state of mind crucial to

✳ ABOVE: *Remember, luxury comes in small packages, too. A very small entryway table, topped with a piece of white marble, gives even the most modest foyer a grand feeling—and it's a very useful surface as well.*

✳ OPPOSITE: *High-quality, sophisticated taffeta and lace transform a round, particleboard table from ordinary to high-end.*

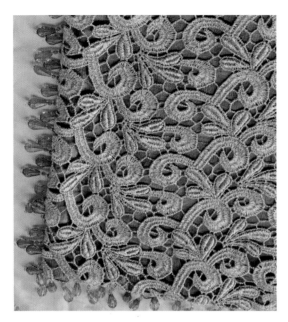

romantic style: enjoying the beauty around you, taking time to linger in the bath, savoring a leisurely dinner or a glass of brandy by the fire after a long day. Luxury does not have to be expensive, but it can be. The Venetian glass wall sconces, sterling silver candelabra, or cashmere throw are luxurious and costly but worth the price if you can afford them. Such items give years of service and pleasure and can be passed down, creating a double sense of romance for the lucky recipient.

Quality

Always buy the best you can afford—it's better to have one or two great pieces, made well, than a room full of poorly made items. You can live well with less if what you have is made with care. Quality never goes out of style. It lasts forever. Even if your own tastes change, a good piece of furniture will always fit into a design scheme. (Think about it—a modern room can be turned on its head in the nicest way by adding a hand-painted bombé chest to soften severe lines.) Lace table coverings can be transformed into curtains or even a bedspread. Velvet drapery panels can be reworked as a tablecloth, pillows, or a bedspread—or moved from one room to another. This philosophy applies to craftsmanship as well as to materials. A quality paint job lasts a long time. My walls have been painted only once in twenty years. They are a neutral backdrop and look right with whatever I put in the room. Of course, it helps to remember that high-quality items have an actual market value, too: If you tire of your Aubusson carpet or 18th-century English highboy or even a good piece of reproduction wood furniture, you can sell or trade it and get something of equal value. Quality pieces are investments.

✳ OPPOSITE: *A large, beautifully made sterling silver candelabra is certainly costly, but it is also destined to become a family heirloom as it is passed from one generation to the next.*

✳ ABOVE: *The rich texture and color of lace over silk is opulent. Beaded trim adds to its over-the-top appeal. Antique salt and pepper shakers are both whimsical and classic.*

Balance and Proportion

Everything works together in a romantic room. Symmetry and scale are the hallmarks of classic design. Obviously, those qualities can be found in well-designed modern and contemporary furniture. However, the sharp, clean edges and lack of ornamentation that characterize a lot of modern furniture would not always work with the antique and French-inspired style I favor.

There are two kinds of balance: symmetrical and asymmetrical. Symmetry is achieved when equal numbers of objects or furnishings are arranged in mirror image—for example, a pair of tables flanking a fireplace or identical vases filled with the same kind of flowers set on each end of a dining table. I am partial to symmetrical arrangements, but they are not an absolute of romantic style. Indeed, many romantic styles, such as baroque, favor asymmetrical arrangements and ornamentation wherein odd numbers of objects or furniture

in varying but related sizes are arranged in a pleasing fashion. An asymmetrical setting is more difficult to achieve than a symmetrical one is, but the challenge of symmetry is to keep it from looking stiff or flat, which can happen if you duplicate items on both sides of a focal point. Avoid a static feel by varying the accessories that adorn the top of matching tables flanking a focal point, for instance. Stack art books on one table and a collection of boxes on the other. Matching chairs can be covered in different fabrics in coordinating patterns or colors.

Proportion refers to the size of objects and their relationship to one another. It's especially important when putting together an asymmetrical arrangement. For example, a small low chair looks out of proportion placed next to a grand piano. It is better to place a larger chair next to the piano and the smaller one nearby so the larger chair buffers it from being overwhelmed by the piano. Yet it's not as simple as "large goes with large" and "small goes with small." Sometimes

the juxtaposition of a small object next to a large one is pleasing if the color palette and texture are similar and create a natural relationship between them. For example, the small chair could look pretty at the end of a grand piano if they are both painted in a similar style. The only way you can really learn what works is by trying different arrangements and color schemes.

The proportions of a room help determine the size and number of furnishings it can hold. A very large room with a few small-scale furnishings placed in its center looks unfurnished and uninviting. Conversely, a small room crammed with oversize pieces looks like a forgotten storage area. Yet one large piece in a small room might look pretty—and perfect.

Monochromatic Palette

I talk more about color in Chapter Two, but for now I would like to say that the palette of romance is a soft, muted one, especially as it relates to the backgrounds in a room—the walls, ceiling, and floors. Tone down bright or deep colors to give rooms a fresh, new life and a background that does not compete with furniture and accessories. That makes romantic style modern—natural colors take the old-fashioned, stuffy feel out of a traditional room. A muted palette also lets the form and silhouette of objects and furnishings take on an importance that might be lost by the use of bright or bold colors.

Texture

Texture engages light and shadows to create interest and movement and spark the senses. Lace, velvet, satin, taffeta, mohair, cashmere, silk, embroidery, needlepoint, tapestry, brocade, crisp linen, damask, Venetian plaster, waxed surfaces, carved wood, polished silver, aged bronze, weathered stone, honed marble—the variety of textures in the romantic portfolio is rich and interesting.

Designing and decorating a home is an emotional adventure—as exciting as any ocean voyage. It can be, if you let it. Don't be overwhelmed. See where your dreams take you—make note of them. I am inspired by whatever I am doing or wherever I am. So much of my design work and inspiration happens when I am out and about, browsing in fabric stores, strolling through a gallery or museum, or even shopping downtown. My eyes are wide with all that the world has to offer. Tune in to your senses and trust your instincts: If it feels right, take a leap of faith and indulge yourself.

✳ OPPOSITE: *Soft cream in many subtle shades creates the perfect romantic palette, soft and monochromatic, in my music room. Note also how everything is in scale. The piano would look imposing in a small room, but here, in front of the large bay window, it looks right at home. The flowers add height to the instrument and are in sympathy with the height of the draperies. The small love seat is often pulled to the side of the room to allow for stand-up cocktail parties, but its small size is not thrown off by the piano, because they are in the same color family.*

✳ ABOVE: *Notice how the morning light bounces off this pretty brocade, giving it a whole other look than it has in evening candlelight.*

Chapter Two

BEAUTIFUL BACKGROUNDS

Elegant furniture and well-chosen accessories are the "jewels" that make a romantic room sparkle. But what about the outfit they adorn? Before you choose the right accessories, you need to slip into the perfect dress. Similarly, you should be able to walk into a room that is empty of furniture, rugs, and window treatments and say, "This is a beautiful space." Only after a room's walls and ceiling are painted and trimmed, its floor is finished or treated, and doorways and windows are enlarged or replaced, can you begin to add and layer furnishings, lighting, and textiles.

My house is an 1889 Queen Anne–style Victorian. Even though French and Italian furnishings and decoration of the 17th and 18th centuries inspire my personal style (updated and lightened to suit my preference and practicality, of course), I never felt the need to change the essential architecture of the house. It was love at first sight. Of course, I wanted to put my style stamp on the Grande Dame. Her exterior was already painted in a creamy white instead of the more predictable "painted lady" tactic of putting a different color on individual gingerbread features. When a visitor walks up the steps to the front door, they have a hint of what to expect once they cross its threshold.

The interior was another story altogether. It was a warren of small, dark rooms. The previous owner, film director Francis Ford Coppola, and his family favored the deep, dark colors normally associated with Victorian style, along with some modern items such as neon lights and wall-to-wall gray carpeting that didn't fit into my vision. Underneath the heavy woods and dark colors, the interior had all the beautiful, romantic features

I look for—high ceilings, many windows, interesting moldings, and ornate fireplaces. In other words, the house had "good bones." I knew that certain interior characteristics could be improved without eliminating the intrinsic charm of the house.

I had several walls on each of the home's four floors removed to create open space so the light from the windows would reach into the core of the house. Deep Victorian town houses, whether

✵ ABOVE: *This is the way my music room looked in the 1950s—very different from my style but still very warm and inviting.*

they are detached like mine or attached on either side or both, are often dark in the middle, since the main source of natural light comes from the back and front. (The solution I used can be applied to any home that has smallish rooms.) For example, walls and a narrow door closed off the original entryway. I had the walls removed and the entryway opened up into a wide, high arch so now you can see all the way through to the other end of the house and the garden. I enlarged other doors and windows. I then lightened the interior walls with a rich glazing technique, which

✷ BELOW: *The French doors in the dining room were originally lower, with standard square corners. I replaced them with large, arched versions— very dramatic!*

✷ OPPOSITE: *I found old French doors and had them retrofitted to use in my master bathroom's shower and water closet. It took some effort, but the lines and soft color of the old wood fit my vision. Beautifully detailed architectural elements like these doors can have many lives and uses. I could have just as easily used these doors in any room of my house. They were originally used in a Paris shop.*

shows off moldings to full advantage. When the eye is not torn in different directions by a lot of patterns and colors, pure form and lines become more apparent and can be appreciated.

There are no straight, contemporary lines in my rooms. It's a symphony of feminine, curvy lines. You don't see any plain flat paint on my walls; instead, glazes and hand-painting add depth. As you go through life, you see things dif-ferently, and I see now with a softer eye. I tend not to like anything stark and bright, defined with hard edges. I like soft curves. They are a part of the design foundation of all the homes that I love. Gentle sweeping lines are welcoming and comfortable—they draw you in. Think about it in terms of a garden path. A straight walkway lined with uniform rows of bricks is not as inviting as a winding path covered in rounded cobblestones.

Open for Romance

If you are able to move or remove walls and raise the ceiling height in your home to create large spaces, consider it. Open, airy rooms define Old World romance. They recall the large reception halls and ballrooms found in the castles and chateaus of Europe—my home is like a little castle on a hill, with its 13-foot ceilings and connecting rooms. High ceilings lend instant grandeur to any space. Raising the ceilings in your home even a foot or two makes a dramatic difference and certainly makes standard-size rooms feel bigger. New homes can be designed to include 12-foot ceilings instead of the more conventional 8- or 9-foot heights.

If you can't undertake such major construction (knocking out walls and ceilings does make a temporary mess of things and is an investment of money and time), small rooms can be made grander and more romantic by widening and raising doorways and entryways and by enlarging windows. Doors and windows in most homes are on the small side. Larger openings give more presence and stature to a room and literally open up spaces, especially those between a hallway and a room and between adjoining rooms. They also bring in more light, both natural and reflected.

Scale must be considered when making anything larger—a wall-size window or oversize door can make a room in a small cottage look off balance. Be careful when judging how large you can actually go. Use some blue painter's tape to mark off possible window and door sizes. If the room feels dwarfed by the "opening" you created, it's too big. There are no hard and fast rules—how does it feel to you? On the other hand, a row of floor-to-ceiling windows can make a small room into a sun-filled garden or breakfast room. My small garden room doubles as an intimate dining space. It has floor-to-ceiling windows and a glass ceiling, and it's all in perfect scale because the windows are narrow and paned.

This is where the advice of an architect or designer comes in. He or she can be hired hourly for a reasonable price to consult on a small project (or commissioned to take care of a major decorating job from start to finish) and tell you exactly how wide or large a door or window can be without throwing off the scale of your room. For example, if you have two rooms, a living room and a dining room, adjoined by a small opening,

※ BELOW AND OPPOSITE: *These windows in a bay off of my garden room were an original feature of the house. They make the small nook feel very airy.*

you can raise the doorway almost to the ceiling and widen it to leave only a couple of feet on each side, and perhaps even arch it for a softer look. Or replace a single door with a double door. The panels of the double door do not have to be the width of a full-size door—they can be made slightly narrower to fit a small space, but the effect is that of a grand entrance.

Changing plain doors to paneled versions is also very Old World and romantic. Exquisite old, solid wood-paneled doors can be found at salvage and antique shops for a one-of-a-kind look. A carpenter will no doubt be required to retrofit the doors into place, but it's well worth the effort. It is hard to find new doors of the same quality today without paying a high price. If you are building a new house in a romantic style, why not purchase old interior and exterior paneled and glass doors for it? It costs no more to create openings for old

doors than it does for new ones when building from the ground up. How lovely it is to have some history and charm built right into a new house. And you can be assured that no one on your block will have the same thing.

Etched interior windows and French doors leading from one room to another also open up a space and frame views without having to remove walls—these features needn't be reserved for exterior walls. French, or glass-panel, doors visually enlarge spaces and certainly bring in more natural light. I love frosted glass panels in

❊ OPPOSITE: *The door leading from the hallway to the music room used to be low and square. Now it's wide, tall, and curved and helps bring even more light into both spaces.*
❊ ABOVE: *Stained glass and leaded glass windows found at salvage shops and antique stores bring Old World appeal to a home.*

doors—they introduce light without sacrificing privacy. Floral designs and undulating patterns are also romantic and filter light and shadow in playful ways. I use a lot of clear, etched beveled glass in the doors of my house.

Colored and stained-glass windows were popular in the Victorian era; there were a lot of examples in the house when I moved in. The only problem is, they don't let in much light. I saved only three colored leaded-glass windows and replaced the others with clear and frosted white pieces of glass so I can enjoy the northern light coming through them in the morning. Most of the etched glass panels in the house were made to order. You can etch your own glass panels; it's not as difficult as it sounds (see page 172 for how-to).

My house has many different kinds of windows—there is no reason that every window in a home has to be uniform, as long as the overall effect on the exterior of the house is pleasing. Suit the window style to each room. Bay windows are wonderful in bedrooms. A plain living room window can be replaced with an interesting floor-to-ceiling Palladian style. I love harlequin windows as well. All three look beautiful from the curb.

✳ TOP: *The transom above a door in my kitchen brings in light to the somewhat dark room.*

✳ BOTTOM: *Etched and frosted glass is a perfect solution for rooms where there are no view or privacy concerns—they still let in light, but do so discreetly.*

Hardware

Don't neglect grates, switch plates, hinges, doorknobs, and pulls. Replace ordinary fixtures with handmade, vintage reproduction, or one-of-a-kind flea market gems to immediately add unusual style, history, and romance to a door or window. Hardware does not have to be heavily ornamented to be beautiful. Simple beaded brass and clear faceted glass doorknobs, hand hammered wrought iron pulls and latches, and gold-plated cremone window bolts add further sparkle and glamour to what would otherwise be solely utilitarian items.

CREMONE BOLT

A device applied, from top to bottom, to the surface of a window or door surround that locks the door or sash into the frame by a turn of knob or lever.

Moldings

Elegant moldings give a room presence and architectural detail. They bring dimension and texture to flat expanses of walls. The walls in my home are so elaborate that I don't need to further accessorize with art—the walls are the art. For example, I have an entire room adorned with arched, mirrored panels surrounded by decorative moldings; it has a very 18th-century look. A second living room features four panels (also known as *friezes*) from the famed designer Elsie de Wolfe's collection. She is the woman credited with inventing the business of interior decoration in America in the early part of the 20th century. Her book, *The House in Good Taste*, published in 1913, extolls the virtues of paneled walls and use of moldings—advice that is as fresh and useful today as it was then. You can create the feeling of Elsie de Wolfe–style friezes by attaching a variety of wood or plaster forms and figures to your wall inside panels created from molding.

Consider replacing narrow baseboards with 5- or 6-inch molding. If your room has high ceilings, add a thick rail about 1 or 2 feet from the floor to give a room an estate look (an unconventional and uncommon use of moldings in today's homes, but customary in large estate houses in England)—or place the chair rail at the standard 3- or 4-foot height and add picture-frame moldings below it for a paneled effect. Or you might choose to forgo the chair rail in favor of large panels created with picture-frame molding and center medallions for a French chateau or Italian palazzo look (see page 164 for details on how to add picture-frame molding and medallions to your walls). *(continued on page 36)*

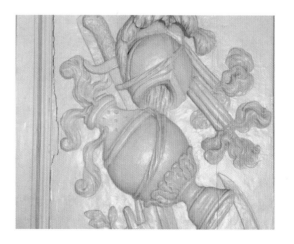

RINCEAU

An ornamental device found in molding and on furniture composed of intertwining stalks of acanthus leaves and other foliage.

✳ OPPOSITE: *These panels, from the collection of famed interior designer Elsie de Wolfe, were found at auction. The cracks you see are a testament to their survival of the 1989 earthquake.*

✳ ABOVE: *Molding and wooden appliqués were applied to plain bedroom walls, then given an antique washed effect with paint, which makes them look as if they've been there since the 1900s.*

You can also have picture railing added 2 feet from the ceiling to visually lower a high ceiling in a small, narrow room. The molding on the wall is placed 12 inches from the ceiling's perimeter. This trick makes a high ceiling look lower. Continue the wall paint treatment onto the ceiling to create the look of a high ceiling. Traditional crown moldings are elegant when attached to the top of the wall, but proceed with caution if you have low ceilings: The molding can visually minimize the ceiling height and make it appear even lower.

Salvage yards and specialty Web sites are good resources for vintage moldings (and other architectural details such as columns and cornices) in styles (commonly referred to as "profiles" in the design and building trades) no longer manufactured. You can also bring a fragment of molding to a woodworker or carpenter, and he or she can create custom moldings based on an old pattern—but this is extremely costly. When my architect and designer started to add more moldings to the existing trim, many had to be made to order, either of wood or plaster. Since that time, I have noticed that there are many ready-made wood

and polyurethane moldings available that let you achieve a custom look without the custom price tag. Their high level of detail is quite authentic. The interest in using moldings and other architectural features (corbels, ceiling medallions, columns, etc.) in homes has encouraged molding manufacturers to expand their offerings and reintroduce previously discontinued styles. As a result, there is a tremendous choice in ready-made moldings, so you are bound to find what you like.

BOISERIE

Ornate and intricately carved wooden panels used on walls and furnishings popular in France during the 17th and 18th centuries. The earliest examples were left unfinished, but later the panels were gilded or painted.

Fireplaces

What's more romantic than a crackling fire? In San Francisco, the weather is temperate and often wet, so a fire is a welcome addition practically all year-round. Even when it's too warm to burn wood, the grandeur of a fireplace surround lends an air of romance to my rooms. All the fireplaces on the parlor floor of the house are made of wood and have rich scroll and shell carvings, done by a talented master craftsman. They have all been covered in paint finishes that mimic stone. Rococo-style Trumeau mirrors crown the fireplace surrounds in my two living rooms. An Austrian mirror, complete with carved birds, makes the fireplace in my dining room a truly dramatic focal point as well as a perfect place to arrange accessories. Upstairs in a guest room, the

fireplace is an original soft gray marble example. It was the only one I kept in the house, because it is beautifully and simply carved. The others were just plain marble.

If you can't afford to commission a custom carved surround, vintage or reproduction versions can be found fairly easily. In this day and age, they make so many terrific carved fireplace surrounds, many coming from the Orient; you'll probably be overwhelmed trying to choose among them. Salvage yards and large antique malls often stock carved wood fireplace surrounds, including attached mirrors and shelves, removed from old houses. It is a fairly simple job for a carpenter to replace a plain fireplace surround with one you've found.

Vintage and antique stone fireplaces are somewhat harder to come by in the United States and are more easily found in Europe, where they were more commonly used. Sending them across the ocean can be an expensive challenge, since they are so heavy. It requires the help of an experienced shipping firm to ensure the safe transport of the three or four or sometimes more heavy sections of a stone surround. Instead, seek out American vendors who specialize in imported stone architectural details from Europe. They

※ ABOVE: *The crane details on this rare 17th-century European mirror are lighthearted. Mirrors such as this one are extremely hard to find, but you can create a luxurious looking glass by framing a piece of mirror with fancy carved molding and covering it with gold or silver leaf. If you do so, be sure to burnish the surface of the metal with a soft cloth to give it a soft, aged appearance.*

※ OPPOSITE: *This ornate fireplace surround only looks antique—it was made especially to fit the space by a local master carpenter and painted to achieve the look of stone and to match the antique mirror that hangs above it. A mantel this incredible holds its own and needs only a pretty clock as an accessory.*

ship items in bulk, and while these items are still costly, buying them from an importer could be less expensive than trying to ship a special item on your own.

Luckily you can find reproduction stone fireplaces today, many based on actual pieces found in chateaus and mansions, and these good-quality examples can be as beautiful as the genu-ine article. Even if you don't have an actual fireplace in your room, a mantel, mantelshelf, or surround can be mounted to the wall to create a lovely "fool the eye" effect. Place candles or a large bouquet of flowers in front of it, where the natural opening for the firebox would be. Continue your illusion by placing an ornate screen or a set of whimsical andirons in front of the surround.

✳ CLOCKWISE FROM ABOVE, LEFT: *A carved and painted mantel, a pretty fireplace screen, and fancy andirons are details that truly make your fireplace a major focal point. Look for antique fireplace accessories at auctions and estate sales.*

Floors

Floors are an important but often forgotten decorative element of a room. They don't have to be plain; they can be adorned with hand painting or stenciling. If the floor has ornamental touches, it does not need to be covered with a carpet. I don't cover my painted floors with rugs, although I use them in some rooms where the floors are simply bleached and not painted. If you plan on painting your wooden floor (see page 170 for a simple floor-painting project), consider creating a 5- or 6-inch border around the room or an all-over pattern of small flowers or ribbons. A center medallion on a wood floor entryway would be very welcoming. Use a palette of soft colors that complement the rest of your décor.

Most of the floors in my house are wood. I like the bleached parquet styles found in the two living rooms; and the hand-painted floors, such as those in my bathroom and dressing room, are my favorite—they feature beautiful cherubs and flowers painted in pale rose and lavender. If you are not skilled at hand-painting, you can use stencils, decals, or decoupage to add detail around the edges of an otherwise plain floor or on the corners or where heavy traffic won't mar

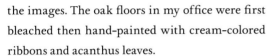

the images. The oak floors in my office were first bleached then hand-painted with cream-colored ribbons and acanthus leaves.

I am not fond of wall-to-wall carpeting because of the upkeep—with three dogs, it is not practical—but I understand that many people have carpeting in their homes. If you have wall-to-wall carpeting, area rugs are beneficial in defining seating areas. Use room-size rugs to cover large expanses of carpeting you don't love, until you have the time and funds necessary to replace the carpeting with wood or tile.

Beautiful tile and stonework flooring is very romantic and charming. I have large 8- by 8-inch antique terra-cotta chateau tile in my kitchen. It just gets better with age. Nowadays you can find importers who bring in old limestone and quarry tile floors from castles and old homes throughout Europe—this is an extravagance, to be sure. Yet it is marvelous to walk on something that kings and princesses and scoundrels may have scurried across ages ago. Another option is to use terra-cotta tiles from Mexico, which are reasonably priced and look authentically aged; affordable ceramic tiles made to look like old stone; or readily available slate imported from India.

The floors in my entryway and garden room are inlayed with four different colors of marble.

This is a more complex job than laying standard square tiles and requires the expertise of a professional to design and install, but the result is dramatic. The entrance to my house is ample but not enormous, yet the floor, soaring ceiling, and sweeping staircase make it seem grand and welcoming. Since my marble floors are polished and sealed on a regular basis, they are stain- and scuff-resistant. Ceramic tile, made to look like marble or another stone, is an affordable alternative. Add a ready-made center medallion to a room and surround it with a simple coordinating tile to achieve the feeling of an inlaid floor.

PAINT A COLOR STORY

I like color to move from one room to another. It's unifying. I am not partial to the "one pink room, one green room, and one yellow room" standard. Moreover, I do not think bright colors do much for a room. The eye quickly tires of strong colors. Just like in nature, God didn't put orange and lime green in the sky for us to look at all the time. A palette close to nature is good for the eye. Off-white and milky white, cream, beige, gray blue, and pale green make for soothing backgrounds. My house is painted in a series of beige glazes sometimes mixed with green, but it's all soothing and color flows uninterrupted from one area and level of the house to another. Even if one room has a green tinge and another a slightly blue hue, the overall effect is one of soft, pale continuity because the color difference is so subtle.

For example, I combine a light blue gray or a pale pink with the beiges, but all of them are soft so they never look harsh or distracting when placed together. I paint all the moldings in the same tone for a unified, more textural look and so that there are no harsh outlines. As a result, the walls and the moldings look like they have been there for a while and have, over time, just naturally faded to a warm patina. It's a chalky palette, as if seen through gauze. The wall-color story in my home is one reason that the house still feels cozy, comfortable, and soft even though the rooms are of grand scale and the furnishings and fixtures are sumptuous. The creams and beiges keep the opulence in check and create a welcoming ambience.

The background's subtle colors can be used to define and develop the style of each room's furnishings. Even if you use different styles of fur-

niture, you don't have to sacrifice harmony. For example, you can pair a primitive chest of drawers with a more formal carved mirror if the finishes relate to the basic background colors. The rooms always look right and pulled together, because they are focused and related, and they make one statement. Using a neutral palette is an easy way to decorate.

The best way to develop a color scheme is to simply look at a variety of paint chips and decide which ones you like the best. Any color can be softened or muted with the addition of water or with gray, white, cream, or beige paint. Once you have chosen your favorite color and softened it

into a neutral version, select three or four adjacent shades and add them to a basic glaze so they can be carefully layered and blended for depth and texture. This transforms flat drywall into a surface with a lot of light and shadow play—like old castle walls that have aged gracefully over hundreds of years (see page 174 for how to glaze a wall).

It should not come as a surprise that it takes a while to paint walls this way (the ones in my home took several months to complete), but once it's done, it's done. You don't have to change it again. Mine were painted more than twenty years ago, and they all still look fabulous. In fact, I think they look better with age. A neutral background can accommodate changes in furnishings, upholstery, and accessories as well. Romantic decorating doesn't sacrifice practical-

ity for fantasy—a neutral background is practical and versatile.

If you are completely daunted by the prospect of glazing your walls in this manner or cannot afford to hire someone to do it, there is nothing wrong with using wallpaper that accomplishes the same effect. In fact, in the 1800s, wallpaper manufacturers created such glazed or faux finishes on paper, ready for hanging. You can find similar wallpaper today. Instead of floral prints or stripes, the paper closely mimics a glazed, plastered, or even stone surface. Any of these options would be nice alternatives to flat paint, which lacks the depth and warmth of a layered paint effect.

I also love layering painted treatments on top of the glazing. Flowers, vines, and urns overflowing with flora and foliage are painted in

Once the backgrounds in your house are completed, you don't have to worry about them for a very long time. The fun of decorating begins. The best advice I can give anyone who is embarking on creating a romantic home is to take your time. I don't believe in instant decorating. It takes a bit of trial and error to find a good fit. As you develop your decorative eye, you will soon learn what feels comfortable and what doesn't. This takes time and consideration. The romantic features and furnishings of a home should be chosen carefully and should always reflect the personal style and interests of those who live there.

The practical matter of how much you can spend on these features determines what you are able to buy, of course. If your budget is small, invest in the best-made major pieces (sofa, chairs, table) you can afford. Quality over quantity is a smart guideline for any budget, really. A good couch, for example, lasts for many years and can be reupholstered or slipcovered many times over. So spend less on accessories now and upgrade or add later, as finances allow.

The more challenging task is deciding what you like. Today, we're inundated by choices. Sorting through all that is available is a daunting process. Don't let the kaleidoscope of options freeze your design process or frighten you away from change. Make a list of all the rooms you have walked into that made you say, "I want to visit with a friend here or sit down and read a book here," or conversely, "I cannot wait to get out of this place!" Or consider rooms you have seen in interior design magazines and books. Which ones did you love; what rooms resulted in a quick turn of the page? By evaluating and comparing other spaces, you can start to define your own style and identify common decorative themes and elements.

When I see rooms or objects I like, I make it a point to remember them. The strong likes and dislikes are important, but don't spend too much time on middle-of-the-road stuff. Immediately get rid of what you dislike and concentrate on what you love. If you don't absolutely adore something, don't put it into your home. I want to be surrounded by beauty—if an object is not beautiful, it doesn't come through the front door. Just remember: It takes time to create a beautiful home—I always start with one room at a time.

THE SOCIAL HOME: LIVING ROOMS

I refer to the two living rooms on the main level of my house (adjoining "parlors" is a common feature of Victorian houses) as the music room and the drawing room, respectively. Naming rooms is just part of a playful, romantic way of thinking. The music room faces the street and is the closest to the front door; the drawing room is in the center of the house and connects to the music room through a wide entryway. No matter what you call the more formal, public spaces in your home, they should be inviting and exude a sense of ease and happiness. It's a funny thing about living rooms: The more personal and the less generic they are, the more comfortable they are for you and for others.

CHOOSING FURNITURE

Furniture is not like fashion: While clothing goes in and out of style and season, furniture should last for many years. Sofas can be reupholstered numerous times if their frames and construction are solid. I reupholster the sofas in my living room every eighteen months, which I understand is not practical for most people. I love changing textiles frequently, and I also have three large dogs. Much as I adore them, they cause a lot of wear and tear on the upholstery in my house. It also demonstrates the fact that a well-made piece of furniture lasts forever and can be reinvented many times over. In fact, most of the furniture in my house has been with me for twenty-five years, some of it still covered in the original fabric. Antique furniture should be intact and solid (no wobbly or loose legs or drawer fronts), and new furniture should be made from kiln-dried hardwoods like mahogany and oak or, if made from pine, fitted together with dovetailed joints and

RECAMIER

A lounging sofa made popular in the Regency period (1811-1820), characterized by a visible wooden frame and curving arms usually decorated with brass inlay. One arm is always higher than the other, making it perfect for reclining. The chaise was named after Madame Recamier, who would receive male visitors while stretched out on the chaise.

nails or pegs instead of staples and small finishing nails. I use pillows, accessories, draperies, and flowers to change the feel of the room season by season.

Many sofas and chairs are comfortable to sit on, but which comfy models are right for your room? Size is important. Antique chairs or those that are accurately based on antiques are often petite, because people back in the day were smaller. There was no such thing as oversize furniture in the 17th and 18th centuries. Diminutive vintage furniture can be used decoratively or as occasional pieces. However, if you want a French or English antique look for the main pieces in a room, you could be better off using reproductions, including brand new pieces and 19th- and early 20th-century copies of 17th- and 18th-century originals, all sized to provide modern-day comfort.

✳ ABOVE: *Even antique chairs can be comfortable, especially when the cushion is filled with down and the fabric is soft damask.*

Furniture size as it relates to room proportion is another consideration. I see so many overstuffed sofas and "chair and a halves" on the market, and they always seem to be too big for the rooms they are in—even when they are placed in large rooms. The proportions are bulky, and there is nothing graceful about them. The arms on these pieces seem to be particularly large but serve no function except to take up space. A sofa should fit in the room without filling it.

A loveseat may offer better proportion and breathing room in a small room. Oversize chairs are hard to deal with because it's difficult to bring all the other items in the room into alignment with their scale—the chair often dominates the room and the arrangement. Look for chairs that match the scale of your sofa. There is no need to buy chairs and sofa as a "suite"—meaning the sets of sofa and two chairs that are made to match (the chairs look like a narrow version of the sofa) and covered in the same fabric. It's much more interesting to mix different pieces of the same scale and unify them through similar fabrics.

As far as the color of visible woods and upholstery fabrics, I tend to like bleached wood, soft maple finishes, or painted woods in pale gray or pistachio green. I would not like a room done entirely in dark mahogany. A room filled with heavy dark furniture feels oppressive. Light colors are optimistic (I am not a member of the "doomed romantic" school). Use dark woods sparingly. For instance, a dark wood desk or chair can provide a pleasing, if restrained, contrast to an otherwise neutral palette. As far as textile color, muted blue greens, pinks, and, of course, creams abound in my living room furniture. The music

CHOOSING UPHOLSTERED FURNITURE

The most important aspect of upholstered furniture is what you cannot see—the frame. The best frames are made from kiln-dried hardwoods. The system attached to the framing that supports the cushion should be constructed of eight-way hand-tied coil springing. A trained upholsterer ties each coil into place with twine and interlocks it with other coils using an intricate set of eight knots. As for the cushions, a combination of natural down and fiberfill or high-density foam makes for plush cushions that bounce back. (Pure down cushions have to be constantly plumped after being sat on.) The manufacturer will provide all the information you need to know about new furniture.

Older upholstery bought at an antique or consignment shop is another story. There's no manufacturer's literature to accompany such furniture. That does not mean you should shy away from these pieces. Their frames are more often than not made from hardwood and are, in fact, better made than many inexpensive new versions. Fabric is easily changed and the stuffing revitalized (if you are lucky enough to find a piece with horsehair stuffing, it should be reused and fortified with new foam and down). Keeping the horsehair stuffing helps maintain the original integrity of an antique piece, and it is firm, providing a durable base for newer stuffing. Springs can be retied and frame joints tightened—resulting in a piece that is well made and uniquely yours.

room sofas, for example, are covered in a cream-colored silk, and the chairs are done in pale blue and green brocade with a woven pattern of small flowers that from a distance almost look like polka dots. Furniture dominates a room by definition. Neutral finishes and fabrics on furniture keep a room feeling airy and open. Boldness and surprise can be added with less assertive accessories—a Chinese blue vase, a green chenille throw, or colorful accent pillows.

BERGÈRE CHAIR

An upholstered chair with exposed curved wooden legs, closed sides, and upholstering on the sides, armrests, seat, and back. The seats are often slightly elongated, making them both elegant and comfortable.

❋ OPPOSITE: *Living rooms in modern homes can be romantic and comfortable—and kid-friendly. Note how the arrangement in this family home, which features pieces I designed for C.R. Laine, is welcoming and relaxed yet still very romantic and feminine.*

LIVING ROOM ARRANGEMENTS

The most romantic and practical furniture arrangement is one that allows for easy conversation. I have the tremendous advantage of high ceilings and large rooms. The proportions allow for uncluttered conversation areas that accommodate both large and small groups as well as extra furnishings, such as console tables, occasional chairs, and accessories. Even when I am by myself, I never feel overwhelmed by my two adjoining living rooms. They are set up in a very 18th-century French, very balanced way. They are not just thrown together. There is symmetry about them in the way the color schemes and furniture arrangements complement each other—they do not compete for attention.

In your own living room, furniture can be arranged to accommodate different-size groups, no matter the size. Resist the temptation to line the walls with furniture, leaving the center of the room bare. Bring the furniture into the room. If room size offers no alternative than to place a sofa against one wall, side chairs should flank it closely rather than be pushed into the opposing corners of the room.

If you are fortunate enough to have a fireplace, that makes a natural focal point. In a very large room, two sofas can face each other running perpendicular to the fireplace, with chairs placed on either side of the fireplace, facing the firebox to form a "U" with the sofas. In a medium-size living room (16 by 20, for example), one sofa that fits three people comfortably placed facing the fireplace, with two chairs on either side of the fireplace, is ideal.

I love symmetry, as I've said, but when everything matches too closely, a room feels stiff. In

any size room, the chairs flanking the fireplace and the sofa can be in a different style but unified by upholstery. Sofas look best when upholstered in a fabric that coordinates with the fabric on the chairs.

Side tables and a center coffee table can be placed next. I use two short, large architectural stone plinths (also known as pedestals) in my living room, instead of the conventional long coffee table. But a single coffee table would also work.

Once these basic pieces are in place, other pieces can be added around the room, as space permits. For example, in the more formal music room, a beautiful Pleyel piano made during Mozart's time (he played one exactly like it) is positioned near the window so whoever is playing can take advantage of the view. This placement also creates a stage for the pianist, as the seating area is adjacent to the piano.

My less formal main living room, which I call the drawing room, demonstrates another arrangement possibility. It's the room where I sit in the evening, usually around seven o'clock, after I have changed into something comfortable. I look at the mail, talk with my dogs, and

enjoy a glass of wine and some cheese. The dogs love to kiss me and nibble on some cheese, too, as they lay on the sofa next to me.

The two floral chintz-covered sofas in the drawing room are placed in an "L" formation in front of the fireplace. The fabric brings color to the room and offers a break in the formality of the space. Two custom-made cabinets flank the fireplace. I keep favorite books piled on top. The doors conceal drawers, where I keep family photos. Four angel plinths support a large center octagonal stone slab with beveled edges. Large round tables sit on each side of the sofa facing the fireplace. Armchairs placed opposite one sofa complete the "U" around the fireplace.

A desk placed near the window, which I call the Godfather Desk (because that's the spot Coppola kept *his* desk), is filled with lots of family photos in an ever-changing array of frames. It also holds the telephone and a lamp, along with other small accessories. I'd like to point out that while the desk looks like an antique, it was made new for this spot. The finish is an antique green with touches of gold; the leather top has been replaced several times, because the sun fades and dries it out. Console tables flank the window in the room. They were once one table that was cut in half, and each half was bolted to the wall. Assorted bergère chairs fill in the perimeter of the room and can be pulled into the conversational "L" when more than a few guests stop by. In rooms smaller than mine, a pared-down grouping, including a sofa and chair "L" arrangement with one side between the two and a coffee table, would provide ample seating and practical surfaces without overstuffing the space.

If you don't have a fireplace, a window serves as a lovely focal point, especially if it frames an

interesting view. The arrangement can follow the recommendations just given. If no beautiful view or fireplace exists, create a focal point with architectural details such as a faux fireplace, a hand-painted mural, or a large mirror surrounded by a thick frame painted in the same way as

✳ ABOVE: *My Pleyel piano is just like the one Mozart used for composing. It's the star of my music room.*

✳ OPPOSITE: *A desk placed in a living room is useful for writing letters or checking e-mail, but it's also a lovely surface to hold photographs and personal mementos.*

your molding or gilded in a soft gold, bronze, or silver.

THE ROMANCE OF FABRIC

Fabric alone creates romance in a room not only because of the color and softness it adds, but also because it appeals to our sense of touch. A fabric that feels good is an added bonus. A couch with simple lines goes from starkly modern to luxurious and glamorous when covered with a sumptuous brocade or sleek silk cover. Velvet and tapestry pillows take a tobacco brown leather club chair into a more fanciful and romantic realm. Here are descriptions of some of my favorite romantic fabrics:

Brocade: This is an interwoven design of raised figures or flowers generally made of silk, rayon, and nylon yarns. Sometimes metallic threads are added to the weave for a bit of sparkle. Use it on chairs, accent pillows, and table coverings. Brocade is also known as jacquard.

Chintz: Cotton fabric is "glazed" with a coating of fabric sizing to give it sheen. If you wash chintz in a standard washing machine, the sizing will be removed and the sheen lost, so it must be dry-cleaned. Chintz is often printed with floral designs. Use it to upholster sofas and chairs, for slipcovers, to cover pillows, and as drapes and table coverings. Use floral prints in small doses in the romantic room to bring in a shot of color.

Damask: Damask includes silk, wool, linen, cotton, or synthetic fibers woven in an ornamental repeating pattern normally in the same or similarly colored threads for a low-contrast pattern. The term originally referred to silk fabrics from Damascus, which were elaborately woven in different colors. Use damask on chairs and for table coverings, pillows, draperies, and bed lin-

ens. It is sometimes referred to as a jacquard, as is brocade—although damask is a flatter and lighter weave than brocade.

Silk: Silk is made from a natural filament fiber produced by the silkworm to make its cocoon. Most silk is collected from cultivated worms; tussah silk, or wild silk, is a thicker, shorter fiber produced by worms in their natural habitat. All silk comes from Asia, primarily China. Silk is available in a variety of weights—upholstery-weight silk is heavier than the fashion-weight silk from which scarves and blouses are made. Silk also comes in a variety of finishes, from shiny satin to rustic matte finish "shot" silk, where some threads create bumps in the fabric. Use the upholstery-grade silk of sofas and chairs for draperies, pillows, and bed coverings.

Taffeta: This is a lustrous, medium-weight, plain-weave fabric with a slightly ribbed appearance. It provides a crisp, sometimes stiff, body. Silk taffeta gives the ultimate rustle and pouf, but rayon is an affordable alternative. Use taffeta for luxurious drapes and table coverings.

Tapestry: Tapestry is a form of textile art. Originally, tapestries were all woven by hand on a loom, although a lot of commercially available tapestry today is manufactured on large mechanical looms. Many tapestries depict scenes that include figures and animals or still lifes. Tapestry can be made from silk or wool, as well as man-made fabrics. Use tapestry for pillows and bed coverings or hemmed as wall hangings.

Toile de Jouy: This playful fabric was originally made in the village of Jouy-en-Josas, near Paris. Now most fabric manufacturers create cotton toile, so it is widely available in fabric stores.

The designs usually use one color on a solid background to show a charming pastoral scene or motifs from classical mythology. Toile prints done in more than one color are less common. Use toile to upholster side chairs and for drapes, pillows, and bedspreads.

Velvet: Velvet is a tufted fabric where the cut threads are evenly distributed, giving it a soft, smooth feel. Velvet can be made from a variety of fibers, including rayon and cotton, but velvet made from silk is the most luxurious of all. Use velvet for upholstery on chairs and as draperies and pillows.

Do remember that while fabrics used on furniture and draperies need not match, they should coordinate. As a rule, I use upholstery-grade jacquard, velvet, chintz, and silk on furniture. I change curtains and drapes quite often because it's an easy way to change or update a room—and I confess, I adore fabric. I can't resist a new silk or brocade. I always take little swatches of the other fabrics in the room and samples of the wall paint with me, so I can see how each possible choice fits the room. (Your design journal, page 11, is a perfect place to keep track of your choices as well as your new decorating ideas and inspirations.)

I use upholstery-grade cotton floral chintz from Waverly on my sofas in the drawing room. It is sturdy enough for the dogs to lie on, and it adds a shot of color to the otherwise monochromatic room. Notice the details on the skirt—the special corner and center pleats are part of what makes this classic couch special simply because it is a dressmaker's detail that you do not see on upholstery every day. It takes a little extra time and thought to add on to a piece. The fabric on the round side tables is changed frequently—sometimes it's striped, other times it is solid-colored damask topped by a round lace tablecloth. I have also layered the tablecloths with several pieces of similarly

toned brocades and lace, and the story is about texture as opposed to color or pattern. A busy pattern is not restful to the eye. Texture gives movement without distraction. The music room sofas are covered with white silk and have dressmaker details like shirring on the seat cushions and welting along the seams. The bergère chairs are done in a pale jacquard with vines and flowers. Draperies are made from yards of billowing silk. Indeed, the draperies in both living rooms are pale shell pink, cream, or green silk taffeta. I replace them often because silk and the sun don't mix—they deteriorate quickly. Drapes sewn from man-made fibers, such as nylon or rayon, hold up for a longer period of time and simulate the look of silk quite nicely.

Lovely Lace: Lace is a decorative mesh of interlaced threads that are braided, knotted, looped, and turned to make either simple or complicated patterns and raised work. There are many different styles of lace, including Alençon, Chantilly, Spanish, and Venice.

Of course, I love lace—no room is complete without a touch of it, and that includes living rooms. Lace is more lavishly used in the bedrooms and other private areas of my home, but it still has a place in the public spaces—as table coverings and edging on pillows and as sheers under draperies. There is no reason to hide away inherited doilies and curtains. Line a breadbasket with the doily, or use the curtain panel as a tablecloth on top of a solid-colored fabric. Frame an especially unique example or a series of antique

ments. Set in matching, simple frames, they make a graphic statement—even in a modern home. Lace comes in so many forms that it really gives you a lot of opportunity to play with texture. Cotton, silk, and rayon create different kinds of lace—from thick, open crochet work to delicate netting. All of it is beautiful—and since high-quality Asian-made examples are abundant, it is easy to find either by the yard or as piece goods.

✳ OPPOSITE PAGE: *A big bouquet of textiles—this is exactly how I look at fabric when deciding how tones and textures go together!*

✳ LEFT: *Silk, beads, lace—they all blend to create a symphony of texture.*

✳ BELOW: *A small piece of tapestry or needlepoint, especially if it is an antique, adds color and interest to a neutral room in the form of a pillow.*

LIGHTING

As soon as I get home, I always say to Arthur, my butler, "Let's dim the lights so I can rest my eyes." It's so important to have control over the lighting effects in a house. The simplest way is by adding dimmer switches to every light, especially the living room, where light control is so important for entertaining purposes. After a long day at work, it's extremely soothing to sit in a softly lit room. On the other hand, if you are hosting your book group, bright light may be helpful. But a cocktail party or date benefits from a softer glow. Dimmers are absolutely essential if you have a system of flush-mounted lighting, as so many newer homes have these days. The light from halogen spots can be harsh, and dimmers tone down

> ### BOUILLOTTE LAMP
>
> A style originally from the Louis XVI period (when it held candles) that usually has three branches ending in candle cups and one central, often adjustable rod topped off with a tole shade (a metal shade, often painted in black, sometimes with gold or silver accents).

the glare. Installing slightly lower wattage bulbs (75 instead of 100, 60 instead of 75) is yet another way to soften lamp and overhead light. Three-way bulbs give some flexibility to lamps, but not all lamps have three-way switches.

After dimmers, the most romantic lighting in a living room comes from a chandelier. Those in my living rooms are made in Italy from frosted white, opalescent, and clear Murano glass. They are ornamental without being overdone, since they don't have any bright-colored glass crystals attached to the arms. I don't mind their flamboyance, because the color is understated. If I find a chandelier I like and it has colored drops, I would remove and replace them with clear or frosted white versions. I don't put a lot of colored beads and other embellishment on my dresses for the same reason: I like to see the form and material, and I feel the same way about chandeliers.

Sconces are very romantic, especially gold-toned multicandle styles, whether they are electric or not. Mine have both electric bulbs and a place for traditional wax taper candles. It's fairly

simple to have wires run in the walls for electric sconces—they look pretty in the middle of the panel molding or on each side of a fireplace or picture window. Table lamps are useful for tasks such as reading and hand-sewing. Black shades add a touch of sophistication. I especially favor bouillotte lamps and use them throughout the living rooms, including on side tables and the desk. Candlelight is a mainstay of romantic style. I am partial to placing candles in multiarmed candelabras, sconces, and nonelectric bouillotte lamps.

❧ ABOVE: *An intricate ironwork Victorian-era chandelier hangs at the top of the back staircase of my house. It reminds me of a crown—for a princess, of course.*
❧ RIGHT: *One of many brass ribbon sconces I collect. They are the perfect romantic lighting solution to flank fireplaces, beds, and desks.*
❧ OPPOSITE: *The hand-blown Murano glass chandelier in my music room is one of several in my home that I had imported new from Italy.*

MIRRORS

Mirrors, especially old ones, capture the essence of the past within their depths. Reflective surfaces are a must for bringing light and sparkle into any romantic room. I have mirrored walls in my music room, and they give such a shimmer to the space. Sometimes I refer to it as my "Versailles room" because it reminds me of the mirrored rooms in the famed French chateau. During the day, the panels reflect even more of the natural light into the room; and at night, they reflect candlelight and the lights of the city so that the whole room seems to glitter. Mirrored walls do make small rooms appear bigger—that's not a myth. They can have too much of a modern edge if they are not softened with a frame or trim molding. Large hanging mirrors can also brighten and open up a room. Age the glass to add character and a realistic antique finish (go to page 204 for how-to).

Mirrored furniture is another way to bring reflection and glamour to a room. One or two mirrored pieces in a room are all you need. A set of mirrored nesting tables adds subtle lux to a room. Nesting tables are practical, because they can be pulled into service as side tables at cocktail parties when entertaining but be stored away compactly when not in use. A mirrored chest of drawers provides storage—but in such an enchanting way! In a bedroom, the drawers can hold lingerie and clothing. In a hallway, dining, or living room, they can hold linens, silverware, family photos, or games.

✳ ABOVE: *Wall mirrors bring light and sparkle to rooms, but so does mirrored furniture. The set of three nesting tables is very practical, as they stack neatly in the corner of a room when not being used.*

RUGS

I don't have a lot of rugs in my house, but I do use one in the music room (and smaller versions in bedrooms). They add another layer of texture to the wood floor and provide cushioning underfoot, along with further defining the seating area. French carpets are my favorite, especially Aubussons. Needlepoint rugs and Persians in soft, muted tones blend seamlessly with the soft color palette established on the walls and in furnishings.

Old, even gently worn carpets, give a room instant Old World charm. In Europe, rugs are passed down from one generation to the next and just get better and better as they are used. Any deterioration that comes from wear is charming. Colors fade, threads become bare—those imperfections add character and are perfectly acceptable as long as the rug is clean, as ingrained dirt, more than anything, damages rugs. Always take your rugs, new and old, to a reputable cleaning service once a year; and vacuum rugs regularly— at least once a week.

FRENCH RUGS

Aubussons are flat-weave wool tapestry rugs with a central medallion and floral motifs in muted pastel colors, originally made in France in a town of the same name, from the 16th to the 19th century. Savonnerie are woven rugs but have a thicker pile than Aubusson carpets do. They were made in Paris starting in 1628. Designs created by court artists included floral arrangements, military and heraldic references, and architectural motifs. Warps (the yarn of any woven textile arranged lengthwise on a loom and crossed by the woof) were made out of linen, and the woolen pile was woven using symmetrical knots. Authentic Savonneries are much more rare than Aubussons, because they were made exclusively for the French Court and can cost hundreds of thousands of dollars. At the time of production, Aubussons were considered the "poor man's rug," although today they can cost well into the high tens of thousands of dollars.

While French Aubussons are expensive, you can find Oriental and Asian rugs from the 19th and early 20th centuries at surprisingly reasonable prices at auctions and antique stores, simply because so many were made. Look for floral patterns with soft color palettes instead of more standard navy and crimson backgrounds to stay within a romantic vocabulary. Always go to a reputable dealer when making an investment in a rug. The world of rugs is complicated. In general, hand-tufted or woven rugs are better (and more attractive) than machine-made rugs. Vegetable dyes produce soft colors, but synthetic dyes are more resistant to fading.

ACCESSORIES

The trimmings are what give a room personality. Do you like knickknacks or big bowls filled with interesting flowers and other vegetation? Do you collect boxes, clocks, miniature shoes, thimbles, or bronze figurines? Accessories have to be something that relates to your lifestyle and interests, or otherwise they look as if they were placed in a room by someone other than the homeowner, simply for the purpose of matching the other items in the space. I collect boxes and enjoy showing them off in my living room. I have musical figures in the music room because I love music and everything about it. It's nice to be interested in collecting; how wonderful it would be to get your children interested in it, too. Showing off your prized possessions is a good way to pique young people's curiosity about beautiful objects. Assemble items that appeal to you, slowly and lovingly; this is how accessorizing any room should start.

✺ ABOVE: *Boxes are among my most favored accessory for any room but especially the living room, where they hold photographs, playing cards, and the ubiquitous and not-so-romantic television remote control.*

If I would be pressed to say what accessories are essential in a romantic living room, I would include a mantel clock, especially one with ormolu details (reproductions are widely available if an authentic version is out of your financial reach); boxes made from wood, glass, shell, and other materials; bowls filled with flowers; and family pictures in interesting frames. (I don't follow the old-fashioned rule that family pictures should be displayed only in private rooms, such as the bedroom.)

I am especially fond of large pretty boxes where personal mementos can be kept. It's just a marvelous way of reliving a vacation or recalling an evening out on the town. And whenever you look at the box, you are reminded that it contains something special. Say you are in the process of changing your home—keep track of the changes with photographs and notes, and keep them in a box reserved just for that purpose. Or keep a box for each trip you take. Make sure these decorative boxes are accessible, on a shelf or coffee table.

I designed a particular treasure box that has the ambience of Italy. I call it a Tuscan box; it has an ormolu pattern inspired by a fabric I saw that was swirly and curvy. Whenever I travel or shop now, I am always collecting pamphlets or cards, or something from restaurants, or anecdotes that people send me, and I keep them in that box. Every time I look inside, I am reminded of all those places and ideas. It's my "romantic memory."

I imagine a couple having a glass of wine together before dinner, while going through it and laughing and remembering. A box filled with secrets and images like that makes memories very special. As you get older, capturing memories and small but meaningful odds and ends in a box is so important. If you have a child, give him or her a beautiful box for keeping special items in, and store it in the living room. The children will feel important, and it makes them realize what life is about. If you play bridge, you can keep your cards in the box on your game table. There are just so many practical uses for a decorative box (including storage for the television remote control—if you must!).

ORMOLU

This is a gold-toned finish used on less costly metals to imitate gold. The metal is then sometimes made into intricate mountings that are applied to the edges and fronts of furniture, boxes, and clocks. Ormolu mountings are characteristic of 18th-century furniture and clocks and attained their highest artistic and technical development in France. Ormolu was also produced in England. Experts say workmanship deteriorated in the 19th century and by the turn of the century had fallen out of favor.

The Thrill of the Hunt

Shopping for furniture and decorative items at auction is an exciting way to buy. To avoid getting caught up in the excitement (and possible high bidding) of an auction, you must have a plan. Make a list of what you are looking for before you go, and set a limit on how high you are willing to go for a single item. Bid on an item only if you have such a feeling about it that it brings a strong emotion to the surface. If you instantly feel that strongly about something, get it, because you won't see it again. It doesn't happen often that you spot an item that you love at auction, and it's rare you get a second chance at it. For example, it is doubtful that the Elsie de Wolfe panels in my drawing room would have ever come up at auction again. These treasures, previously owned by the famed designer, are one-of-a-kind, and I knew they would add special flair to my living room. When I was first furnishing my home, feelings of excitement about the thrill of the hunt would happen often, because I was actively looking for items. Bid only on pieces that are well made and beautiful, and they will become important pieces in your home and reward you many times over the years.

When arranging accessories, don't worry too much about getting a perfect grouping. Of course, a table should not be crowded with all manner of knickknacks. A box, candlesticks or a candelabra, or a few small, meaningful family photos in pretty frames make a nice collection for a coffee table. Some people like to use trays to corral disparate items, and that can be pretty. I also love to place stacks of fashion books and magazines on side tables. And a vase or bowl full of flowers makes any surface romantic, in my opinion. I adore picture frames, and there are so many reasonably priced, glamorous ones available now that you can play with how you arrange them and change them often.

☀ OPPOSITE: *A collection of small bejeweled boxes can hold small items such as earrings, matches, or even thumbtacks.*

☀ LEFT: *A pink glass egg held in a brass "frame" is actually a container.*

Chapter Four

COOKING, DINING, AND ENTERTAINING

Sharing food with friends or just enjoying a delicious meal by yourself is one of the greatest pleasures of life. Breakfast might be as simple as some tea and toast and fresh berries. Lunch might be a slice of quiche and a salad or a bowl of piping-hot soup. There are cold, wet days when I've worked espe-cially hard that I call Arthur and say, "Macaroni and cheese for dinner!" because comfort food is the only thing that will do. I am inspired by Jackie O's favorite dinner: a salad with all the veg-etables cut beautifully and a baked potato topped with a big dollop of sour cream or crème fraîche and caviar. I'm all for that. For dessert, maybe it's flambé fruit on top of frozen yogurt. Doesn't that sound lovely?

Whether you are serving filet mignon or toast and jam, make it beautiful. Elevate every meal by serving it on your prettiest china. Even when I am dining alone at home, I set the table with lace and linen, light candles, and use my best china. What is the point of having beautiful things if you are not going to enjoy using them? I feel the same way about dining rooms and dining tables—why are they so neglected and forgotten? Why not serve family meals in the dining room? This is a perfect opportunity to spend time with your family, cultivate conversation, and enjoy a civilized meal. It's a chance for children and young people to learn manners and table grac-es that will serve them well throughout their lives. Romantic style doesn't begin and end with furniture and fabrics; it's a way of living and thinking.

As late as the 1950s and 1960s, kitchens were not considered public gathering spaces. They were workrooms, usually confined to the back of a house, the domain of servants and cooks. Din-

ing rooms were reserved for special occasions only. Going further back into time, 17th-, 18th-, and 19th-century kitchens were part of the invis-ible "engine" of town and manor houses and estates, generally located in the basement and run by huge staffs, many of whom were never even known to the homeowner.

Seventeenth- and 18th-century dining rooms were often enormous halls, filled with long tables, numerous chairs, and multiple sideboards. Victorians also tended to entertain on a large scale and always in a formal manner. Standard place settings included twenty-five pieces, each to be used for a specific course. In fact, they had so many utensils and serving pieces for particular food-related circumstances (snail forks, aspara-gus tongs, and tomato servers, not to mention various kinds of spoons and knives) that one full place setting would fill a modern, average-size dining table, although even in Victorian times, a complete service would never be laid for a single dinner.

Today we have a very different view of kitchens and dining rooms. Few among us have a full-time staff to help manage everyday chores or organize large, fancy dinner parties (nor do we have room for them!). Even if we are lucky enough to have a cook or a cleaning person, we tend to spend a lot of time in our kitchens socializing with friends and family. Many modern houses are designed with open kitchens or great rooms; they are an integral part of a family, open for all to see.

The 21st-century kitchen is a public space and functions in a variety of ways. For example, I love to work in my kitchen. I sketch new fashions, review the newspapers, and check my schedule for the day at the long, sturdy wooden table with curved legs that sits in the center of the room. Dining rooms are used less frequently in contemporary life and sometimes are so forgotten that they play the unfortunate role as family catch-all. Actually, a dining room is a wonderful place to enjoy a meal, away from the hustle and bustle of normal activities—and it should be used and enjoyed all the time. Creating a beautiful kitchen and incorporating the dining room into everyday dining, and certainly entertaining, are two ways to enhance the romance of your home.

BEAUTIFUL KITCHENS

Why shouldn't the kitchen be as beautiful as it is practical? Function does not preclude romance, at least when it comes to interior style. Preparing and serving food, sharing meals, or simply enjoying a solo dinner are part of the extraordinary narrative of life.

I enlisted the help of an architect, Diane Burn, to help me create an 18th-century French-inspired kitchen that would perform efficiently in the modern world. In order to create the Old World French ambience I wanted in the kitchen, the room had to be completely gutted. The original layout was cramped and inefficient. It was opened up and reconfigured to provide an easy flow for cooking. I combined many new elements, including cabinetry and appliances, with older pieces such as the market counter that houses the sink to create a truly unique space. I kept Coppola's massive restaurant-quality Wolf stove. When all the burners and ovens are on for a party, the smoke alarm usually goes off, adding to the festivities!

Naturally, Diane and I started with the backgrounds—the plaster walls were distressed

KITCHEN STAFF

In great houses of the 18th and 19th centuries, a fleet of servants ensured that the kitchen ran smoothly. Butlers managed the kitchen staff. The head cook had a team of helpers. Kitchen maids and footmen cleaned fine china, stemware, crystal, and silver. The scullery maid was the lowest-ranking female servant and assisted the kitchen maid by lighting the stove fire and cleaning the floor, stoves, sinks, pots, and dishes.

slightly and glazed in a toasted-butter finish, warmer and a bit darker than the other rooms in the house. As I mentioned earlier, the ceiling was painted in the style of an old French bakery, along with some of the walls.

The windows face a neighboring house and do not provide a very interesting view. To maintain privacy while still allowing light to flood the room, the casement windows were frosted and etched. The double glass doors leading into the hall are covered in lace panels, proving that this delicate fabric is at home everywhere, even in hardworking rooms like the kitchen.

The floors are covered in a terra-cotta tile taken from a chateau; they are virtually indestructible and get better as they age. A kitchen should have something more practical and out of the ordinary than plain wooden floors. Make floors a little more personal through the use of color and texture. For example, use a simple neutral tile and

then use a favorite color as an accent. I like a little square of azure blue punctuating the neutral tiles.

There's no reason that elegant lighting fixtures cannot be used in a kitchen. A chandelier and ornamental sconces provide the practical light necessary in a workspace but still add romance to the room. Baroque sconces on the wall above the sink and flanking windows are festooned with flame-style frosted-glass shades. The large

✳ OPPOSITE: *This large chandelier is another French antique. It came out of a commercial building and had to be rewired and anchored to the ceiling.*
✳ ABOVE, LEFT: *The walls of the kitchen were distressed and painted to look like old, mellow plaster. The sconce is a French antique, once used in a café.*
✳ ABOVE, RIGHT: *I love these terra-cotta tiles. They bring Old World charm and still look great in a modern kitchen.*

bronze-toned chandelier I hung above my long pine table combines Venetian glass shades with arms like vines, a natural form characteristic of the Art Nouveau period. I found it in a Los Angeles antique shop. It was originally in a famous hotel hallway, though I do not recall the name of the hotel, and I liked the look of it for the kitchen because it is so substantial. When my son was young, he had a small party with a few friends on the 4th of July, and some firecrackers went off in the kitchen (by mistake, I'm sure), breaking some of the shades. It's all part of life in an active household. If you want to bring some romance into your kitchen, consider installing a small hanging light with crystal drops above the sink, instead of the more usual flush-mounted schoolhouse lamp or flush-mounted lights. A large crystal chandelier offsets pine or painted cabinetry in a whimsical way. The idea is not to be constrained by conventional definitions of which kind of lighting belongs where.

KITCHEN STORAGE

Even storage, one of the most practical aspects of the kitchen, can be handled in a romantic way. There is no law that says a kitchen has to be completely fitted with built-in, factory-made cabinets. Kitchens of days gone by depended on a variety of storage solutions and hidden pantries to keep food and utensils accessible but neatly and attractively stored. A kitchen has a warmer and friendlier appeal when actual furniture and old pieces are combined with standard equipment and cupboards.

I placed a large antique armoire in my kitchen to hold dishes, silverware, and glasses—I'm told that it came from a farmhouse in France. It is made from pine that was pickled (meaning the finish has a slightly chalky look to it) and has double folding doors operated by cremone bolts. Inside, seven shelves hold almost everything I need to set a beautiful table or throw a festive party. In fact, it's so pretty inside, with all the dishes neatly stacked and the gleaming silverware lined up as if on parade, I often throw the doors open and let them stay that way. All storage does not have to be hidden. Shelves like this are easy to install in any armoire.

A chest of drawers, a china cabinet usually reserved for a dining room, sideboards with drawers, or even an old glass-fronted bookshelf can find new life and add charm to a romantic kitchen. They can hold standard items such as linens and silverware, but they can also stow pots and pans, spices, and cleaning products. Line drawers and shelves with removable felt or rubber shelf-lining material to protect the interior from dings and dust. If the piece you are using is counter height, a piece of stone to fit the top makes a good work surface; marble is especially functional if you do a lot of baking.

If you use an armoire, don't neglect to dress the top of it. I have enhanced mine with a variety of wicker and grapevine baskets, which could provide additional storage if I needed it, but I love them just for their interesting textures. Alternatively, an armoire could be topped with an arrangement of dried flowers or wooden boxes.

My kitchen sink is housed in what was once a wooden counter in a Paris shop. The front of the counter is beautifully carved with shell and floral motifs, in the rococo style. The piece is topped with its original marble (cut to fit the new sink).

☀ OPPOSITE: *This huge armoire may have held linens at one time, although I'm not really sure. Now it holds my large collection of china and silver.*

I love the old stone—chips and stains included. Europeans have been using marble in kitchens for centuries, and the little imperfections are part of the history and romance of the past.

Adding unusual pieces like this to a kitchen scheme is so much more unique and expressive of your individuality than simply using cabinets ordered from a catalog or a showroom. Most carpenters can fit ready-made cabinets around a special item. That is exactly the case in my kitchen—the cabinets to the left of the counter were newly built and topped with a coordinating marble. You don't have to go to France to find vintage commercial items—most large American cities have salvage yards and antique stores that sell and even specialize in these items. If you're really lucky, you might be able to salvage a store fixture yourself from an old shop that is being sold or demolished.

Appliances

Refrigerator, dishwasher, stove—these are some of the necessities of modern life. We can't live without them, but we can disguise them. My ultra-modern Sub-Zero refrigerator/freezer is housed in a pine built-in that mimics the look of the old armoire. It even has handles like those on the other cabinets in the room. The dishwasher is also fitted with a panel, so it fades into the surrounding woodwork. Most cabinet manufacturers offer panels that fit over appliances so they blend seamlessly with all the other doors and drawers.

My Wolf stove is enormous, but I like the way it looks. The hood and exhaust system needed to be

✳ BELOW: *The stainless steel sink is housed in a large counter from a French market. The cabinets on either side were custom built around the impressive piece.*

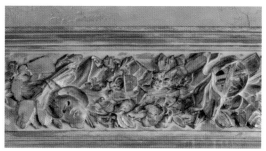

large, since the stove is restaurant grade and quite powerful. I didn't want a stainless steel hood, so I had one custom made. The body of it is glazed in the same paint as the walls. The front carved panel is applied and painted to blend with the boiserie in the rest of the house—the theme is entirely food related. Creating the hood decoration was a major undertaking. You can achieve a similar look without all the fuss by trimming out a plain panel with wood medallions or by hand-painting a decorative motif or mural around the border of the hood. Tiles, especially those that have been hand-painted or have a 3-D effect, can also be used to make this appliance feel less mechanical and more like a part of your cozy, romantic home.

⁂ OPPOSITE: *The stove is big enough to prepare food for large crowds, but we use it every day for making light lunches for one or two, dinner for four or six, or just to pop popcorn for a movie!*

⁂ ABOVE: *The specially made carved detail on the hood displays items that are all food related and include fruit, vegetables, wild game, and even an hour glass to remind me that time is always passing, so don't burn the roast!*

DINING AND ENTERTAINING
Dining Tables and Seating

I have a large dining room with all the usual furnishings: table and chairs and a large dresser (as china cabinets are commonly referred to in England) or buffet for glassware and additional linens. The walls in the room are glazed and painted to look like elaborate molding, with vines and leaves. The floor is inlaid marble. When food service is involved, I think it best to use a flooring material that is easily cleaned and impervious to water. I do not like eating dinner in bright light, so I have dimmers on the large Venetian glass chandeliers above my dining tables. Soft light is kinder to diners, too—it's very flattering.

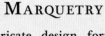

MARQUETRY

An intricate design formed by inlaying any one of a variety of materials cut into small pieces, such as exotic woods, semiprecious stones, or ivory, on a wood or stone surface that is then veneered to another surface, such as a tabletop.

The long Italian oval table in the main dining room has carved legs and a beautiful crosspiece with a sunflower in the middle of it. I had the

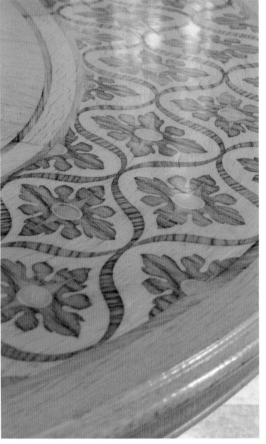

top, which is inlayed with a floral pattern around the edge, refinished and coated with extra-strong polyurethane so spills and food will never damage it. It sits under another spectacular Venetian chandelier that reminds me of an elaborate wedding cake. Matching sconces sit atop the table. The oval-backed upholstered armchairs are covered in an angel-patterned damask in cream and beige tones. I saw the fabric and thought it was so whimsical. The arms and high backs of the chairs make dining and lingering over coffee after the meal has ended so comfortable. If you have a small dining room and are unable to fit chairs with arms on all sides of the table, side chairs with high backs and padded seats are just as relaxing. There is nothing less inviting than uncomfortable dining chairs.

Vintage dining sets are a bargain on the antique market today because many of us have stopped using our dining rooms. If you do have a room reserved for meals, you can find beautifully made furnishings for a small investment. Complete sets are often available, with table, chairs, and sideboard as the usual components. Sometimes sets were broken up among family members, or chairs fell apart and were discarded, or larger dressers and cabinets were sold off and more practical tables were kept when families moved to smaller quarters or when Grandma passed away. So you may have more luck finding orphan dining furniture and putting together an eclectic set.

If this is the case, unify disparate pieces of furniture with a paint glaze (see page 202 for tips on painting chairs; the same technique can be used for any piece of furniture) or light wood stain. A sideboard in a slightly different color or style than a table and chair ensemble can also be very interesting, if the pieces are chosen with a similar finish, style, or scale in mind.

SIDEBOARD

A long, approximately waist-high dining room storage unit composed of drawers sometimes flanked on each side by cabinets with doors.

Table Settings

It's the end of the day, you are slowing down, and the lighting is softer. Or maybe you want to get your day off to a great start with a beautiful breakfast. Creating a beautiful table to match the mood of the evening or morning is part of the fun. I always try to think of an interesting table setting when I have guests. I love layering a table with crisp linen or lace cloths, white embroidered napkins, china in a mix of patterns, flowers—and, of course, candles, especially for dinner parties.

There are many ways you can set the table. Depending on what you are serving, it can be as simple as a plate, napkin, water glass, and knife and fork. Or you can make the table slightly more elaborate with little effort. Here are three classic table settings:

American service: Serving dishes are filled in the kitchen and brought to the table, then passed around the table so guests can serve themselves. After the table is cleared, dessert can either be served at the table or plated in the kitchen and brought to the table. Silverware needed for dessert is brought to the table with the dessert service.

English service: Plates are filled at the table by the host or hostess and passed from guest to guest until everyone is served. Because English service requires a lot of passing, it is best used with a small group of six of fewer guests. All silverware needed for the meal, including dessert, is placed on the table before the meal begins.

Russian or continental service: This is the most formal style. Serving dishes are never placed on the table. Instead, servants serve guests plates of food, one course at a time. Plate replaces plate as one course is removed and another is served. This type of service is often used in fine restaurants and at state dinners.

THE ROMANCE OF TABLE MANNERS

Serve guests of honor and women first, then male guests, counterclockwise around the table. Serve host, then hostess, last. For parties of six or less, wait to eat until your hostess begins. At large parties of eight or more, the hostess urges everyone to begin as they are served.

Aside from being able to set the table in different ways to suit the food and occasion, the other advantage to having an assortment of table linens and china is that you can really match the tone and mood of both your party and the season. For example, a vase filled with red tulips is the perfect centerpiece for a casual dinner party—the table set with French or Italian country pottery instead of bone china. Roses might make an appearance at a more formal dinner party, where the table is set with fine Limoges porcelain china and lots of silver serving pieces.

New linens and laces from the Orient are of a marvelous quality. They are so abundant that it is easy to assemble a nice collection for everyday use. Old lace and embroidered tablecloths are found at flea markets, estate sales, and auctions. In fact, you can find many fine vintage linen and lace table coverings that have never been

TRANSFER WARE

This method of printing on china was developed in England in the mid-18th century. A pattern is etched onto a copper plate, inked, and then transferred to a special tissue that is then laid on top of an already-fired piece of ceramic. The item is glazed and then fired again. The ink is transferred to the piece of china and the tissue is burned away. It was popular to depict country scenes, faraway lands, and botanical images.

used, because the owners were always waiting for just the right occasion to pull them out. That's a shame for them, but not for you. I urge you to use the linens you have and enjoy them. The special occasion is today and every day.

Linen is a strong fiber that gets better—softer and stronger—with every washing, so don't be afraid of it. Wine and food stains can be removed from tablecloths and napkins if addressed immediately or soon after the meal is over, if that's what you're worried about (although what are a few stains among friends; if the dinner was fun, they're worth it). Run cold water through the stain without rubbing it; this will prevent the stain from setting. Then let it soak in warm water and a mild soap. White tablecloths that have yellowish "mystery" stains can be improved by a thirty-minute soak in a sink full of warm water and a cup full of a nonchlorine bleach product such as Snowy or Clorox 2.

PORCELAIN

This hard, white ceramic is nonporous and translucent (you can see your hand behind it when held up to the light). Porcelain was first made by the Chinese in the 7th century by mixing pure white clay and a feldspar mineral called petuntse. In Europe, porcelain was first produced in Meissen, Germany, in the early 18th century, but French and English makers soon followed. Look for place names such as Worcester, Staffordshire, Vienna, Meissen, Sèvres, and Limoges when looking for vintage porcelain.

Iron linens and lace on top of a well-padded ironing board, and place a pressing cloth on top of the fabric. Set the iron on the linen setting for linen and on the lowest setting for lace and embroidery. Do not use starch, as this can degrade the fabric. Always store linens and lace either rolled or lightly folded (avoid making hard creases and never iron creases in—this destroys the fibers).

There is great pleasure in collecting china, too. Odd pieces and entire sets can be picked up for little money in every antique shop in the country. Bring back special pieces when you are on a trip as another way to add to your collection, and you will fondly recall your journey whenever you use them, which I hope is quite often. Don't concern yourself with matching patterns. As long as the dishes are in a similar theme and color (flowers or gold banding, for example), you can mix a set of soup bowls with one set of dinner plates and another collection of salad dishes for a casual meal. Or give each person his or her own dinner plate. When hosting a formal dinner party, however, all dishes should match. This is not a sign of elitism—on the contrary, it is the traditional way of signaling everyone is equal at the dinner table. How nice.

Collecting china is also educational. Get a book on patterns and marks to learn when and where the pieces were made. So many people collect teacups now. I think it's great for a young girl to start collecting teacups, because it provides her with knowledge, focus, and fun. Eventually, she can make her collection into a permanent part of her home. Whenever the cups come out, she will be reminded of so many happy times.

Care for your fine china by hand-washing it in warm soapy water instead of in the dishwasher. Never use abrasives on china, as it is easily

scratched. Hot water can cause or worsen existing "crazing"—those little cracks and lines you often see on old dishes. Crystal goblets and glasses should also be washed by hand.

Candlelight is a necessity at dinnertime as well. The soft glow of white or cream tapers placed in old silver or porcelain candlesticks or candelabras is magical. Avoid scented candles when dining. Their floral or spicy aroma can detract from and even ruin the flavor of the food you have so carefully prepared. Dripless candles are another convenience; they prevent wax from melting onto your fine linens.

❋ OPPOSITE: *These are my favorite wine glasses, light as a feather and handblown. Even inexpensive wine tastes special from these goblets. The etched water glass, while not an exact match, coordinates nicely.*

❋ ABOVE: *Two place settings, one for a formal spring dinner (top), the other for a winter holiday meal (bottom), show how just dishes alone can change the feel of your dining room.*

Flowers

Flowers are very important—no, essential—when entertaining or even when enjoying a family meal. I could not live without flowers. They are cheerful harbingers of springtime and all things fresh and natural—even in the dead of winter. I fill big urns with fresh flowers for parties. When I am not entertaining, I use silk flowers; I have a great source for fabulous faux foliage. Who has time to replace large arrangements every week? Not I.

When guests come, however, fresh flowers are a must. Nothing replaces a real bouquet of flowers. It does not take great floral skill to create a beautiful arrangement. If I want something elaborate, I ask a florist to put together large mixed bouquets. But I also love bunches of heather and big armfuls of baby's breath—both inexpensive and readily available, sometimes at the grocery store or greenmarket, depending on the season. Once the heather is all bunched in the vase, I stick beautiful palm leaves in between or maybe some lavender or a few beautiful lilies. Pink lilies are another one of my favorite flowers—they are so easy to find all year round.

For a more formal look, I make smaller arrangements with the baby's breath by filling small round silver or crystal bowls with the frothy little miniature polka dots and perhaps a few roses. They are so pretty going down the center of the dining table, or on a sideboard or even the coffee table, when you are having a cocktail party.

Flower Arranging— Nature Contained

Flowers fill bowls, vases, urns, glasses, and planters in every room, hall, and passageway in my house. Garden flowers make the most charming bouquets because of their informal, slightly

tousled look. And putting flowers in a room is the best way I can think of to inspire romantic thoughts.

I often have a professional florist make large mixed arrangements, especially when I am hosting a party or other social gathering. However, there are simple ways to display flowers beautifully that don't require the help of a trained florist or a lot of time. If you keep some basic principles in mind, you can fill your house with the sweet scent and delightful cheer of blooms all year round.

There are three ways to achieve a satisfying result with flower arrangements: Stay within the same color palette, but vary the flowers; use the same flower in the same color in a mass grouping; or use a soft background such as baby's breath and punctuate it with a bold flower to create a polka-dot effect. These are all simple strategies

that practically guarantee a beautiful outcome.

In the first, you might mix roses, peonies, ranunculus, and carnations in shades of pink. Roses and peonies are more expensive than carnations, but they are also larger, so you do not need as many; carnations accent the bouquet with their frilly petals. Or you could mix dahlias, mums, and lilacs in shades of purple for a multi-textured effect. White flowers of any kind mixed together and accented with foliage like lemon leaves or eucalyptus are always stunning. Just be sure you have at least three different kinds of flowers when doing a one-color arrangement.

The second method is even easier but, depending on the flower, could be most costly. You need a lot of flowers to make a dramatic statement. I absolutely adore a pottery vase filled with a mass of red tulips or a tall crystal vase overflowing

with long-stemmed crimson roses. Other flowers that look striking in a single-species arrangement are freesias, hyacinths, lilies, carnations, and hydrangeas. You can either use a single color, as I like to do with roses and tulips, or find the same flower in a range of the same tone. For example, a mixture of roses in an array of pink would be so beautiful. A mixed bouquet of hyacinths in springtime shades of pink, white, and purple would shake anyone out of the winter doldrums.

Finally, the polka-dot technique, one of my favorites, is also a snap. Start with a cloud of baby's breath, purple or white heather, or even a burst of foliage like boxwood, fern, or hypericum (which is topped with little orange red berries) and then fill in with three, five, or seven dramatic blooms such as lilies, roses, or tulips. The trick is to choose a flower with structure, something sleek to contrast with the feathery background flower or foliage. For example, a hydrangea may not work as well with the baby's breath because it is a rather elaborate bloom and would blend into the background. It might look nice, but you won't get the playful polka-dot effect.

Select containers with care and creativity. Vases are, of course, the standard. If using a clear vase, make sure the stems of the flowers are attractive, and always trim the leaves from the stems below the water line.

Tulip and gerbera daisy stems are usually free of blemishes; carnation and rose stems aren't as nice. You can line a clear glass vase with a large, sturdy tropical leaf to cover any offending stems (a few days under water will not soften the leaf). But think about all the other containers you can use. Bowls and urns make a theatrical stage for large arrangements. Teacups, eggcups, and tiny etched water glasses are the perfect home for dainty bedside or bathroom blooms. Rustic watering cans, wicker baskets lined with plastic, and old terra-cotta jars make lovely casual containers, perfect for entertaining alfresco or for the kitchen table.

Cherish your dining experiences. It might take an extra few minutes to set the table or wash items by hand (enlist the help of your child or mate and enjoy doing it together), but it is worth sitting down to a lovely table and embracing a moment of simple indulgence. Try it tonight, and see if you don't agree with me.

BALDACHIN

A fabric-covered canopy, classically as a covering over an altar, but the word can now be used to refer to a fabric canopy over a bed. Baldachins can be circular, square, or rectangular.

a bleached finish, or painted a creamy white, for a new lease on life.

I always dress the bed in a lace cover and an assortment of lace-covered pillows. I used the same silk for the bed skirt and the drapes. For extra romance, I draped the bed with a silk and lace canopy that cascaded from a circular baldachin all the way to the floor. It's amazing how much drama you can create with fabric. You can pouf it on the bedposts by tying it with ribbon or leave it loose to cascade gently to the floor.

No bedroom is truly romantic without lace on the windows and bed. For windows, picture delicate beige lace with some soft champagne silk behind it. Beautiful! I recently found some brand-new lace netting in palest peach with a sparkle of silver metallic thread woven into the pattern. The metallic thread gives it an ethereal feeling with a bit of shimmer but without being blatant. Lace like that would be pretty placed in front of a peach-colored silk taffeta and made into drapes, a table covering, or a bed skirt.

✻ RIGHT: *My bedroom is a refuge—calm, comfortable, and simply but beautifully furnished. The textiles in the room are its defining feature, from the beige, shell pink, and foam green Aubusson rug to the cream silk canopy, or baldachin.*

ALENÇON LACE

Alençon is a town in Normandy, France, the original producer of this lace, which is characterized by a background of flowers and swags that are reembroidered along the edges with cording and sometimes beads and pearls. It's often used for wedding dresses, but it also makes a glamorous swag on a four-poster bed or window.

❋ OPPOSITE: *This chest of drawers is one of my favorite pieces in the house. I love the way its rustic charm contrasts with the fancy gilt mirror.*

❋ RIGHT: *The silk canopy panels on my bed can be left to drape straight and pool on the floor (as shown on pages 108–109) or, as shown here, poufed midway down with the help of a ribbon.*

COMPLETELY COZY

Total comfort is key in a bedroom, especially the master bedroom. Luxury starts with the bed, of course. Whatever kind of mattress you like—extra firm or super plush—make sure it is the best quality. A well-made mattress lasts a long time, provides excellent back support, and ensures a good night's sleep. The coil count determines the quality of a mattress. A queen-size bed should have at least 360 coils; a king-size bed, at least 450. Flip the bed over and rotate top to bottom every three or four months to maintain shape and firmness. For extra comfort, add a feather-bed topper. Feather beds are common in Europe and gaining in popularity in this country. They add a cloud of softness on top of the mattress. They should be the same size as the mattress and can be placed either between the mattress cover and the bottom or fitted sheet or on top of the fitted sheet (in which case, they should be protected by a duvet cover).

The rest of the furniture in the room is in the 18th-century French style—bergère chairs, small round and oval bedside tables, a console table where I keep family photos and a bowl of flowers, and an armoire for clothes storage. I always like to have a round table and chairs near bedroom windows. The table is ample enough to hold a vase of flowers and accessories, and it is the perfect place for a light meal for one (or two). And, of course, it's also a delightful spot to sit and read a book, sip some tea, or just enjoy the view out of the window. My table is covered with a creamy silk that puddles on the floor, as well as a lacy cutwork table topper. A collection of small porcelain and enamel shoes parade across the surface, along with some family photos and a vase of whatever flowers are in season. The fauteuil chairs feature a feminine wreath detail along the back.

My favorite piece in the room is also the oldest in the house. I am not sure of the exact date, but the primitive chest of three drawers is probably from the early 18th century. Above it, I hung a French gilt-framed mirror in the Louis style. The combination works beautifully and proves the point that you can mix styles of furniture as long as their palette and scale are in sync.

✳ BELOW: *I created a seating area in my bedroom by covering an inexpensive table form with silk and lace and placing two armchairs on either side of it. A vase overflowing with garden hydrangea, some favorite pictures, and a small pile of current favorite novels completes the scene.*
✳ OPPOSITE: *Arranging pillows on a bed isn't difficult. Start with the largest in the back and work your way forward. As long as the fabrics and lace coverings are in the same color family, feel free to use a variety of lace styles and textures.*

The bedroom is also a good place to further indulge a love of frames and family photos. Photographs of my son, Scott, and my mother are everywhere. I keep little pictures of my sister, my brother and his son, my nephew's children, and cousins in my bedroom and bathroom so I can see them all the time. I love to use them as interesting accents grouped and strategically placed on tables and other surfaces. There are a lot of beautiful new frames you can find that are made of resin yet look just like carved wood. Or you can find plain ones and play with them. Use glue to affix crystals or shells on the frames for added texture and gleam. It's easy to update photos with new ones. It's so much fun to change the frames, too, because it's so inexpensive and there are great frames on the market that are covered with fine beadwork and stardust or glitter. You can also stick with frames made from traditional wood and classic silver. It depends on what kind of personality you have and what you like.

CHANTILLY LACE

Named after the French town where it was first made, Chantilly lace is fine silk, nylon, or cotton netting embroidered with flowers and ribbons. It makes beautiful window sheers.

Electronics and computers are a fact of modern life. The armoire in my room hides a television and stereo system, along with odds and ends I need at hand (pads and pencils, magazines) but don't want to look at all the time. Armoires are so convenient for keeping all the reminders of modern life at bay (or at least out of sight until we need them). Antiques may not be deep enough for conventional televisions, but flat screens fit, and modern armoires are made to order for bulky electronics.

PILLOW TALK

A bed without pillows is like a garden without flowers. Incomplete. Decorating a bed with pillows in a variety of sizes adds visual excitement and texture to the bed. I love mixing different kinds of lace coverings together on pillows—it makes the bed so pretty. Having a variety of pillows is convenient, too. You can shift the pillows around behind your head and shoulders to get just the right comfy configuration for reading, sleeping, or whatever other pleasures you like. Pillows can have any kind of edge, from straight, or "knife-edged," to corded, lace-edged, fringed, or ruffled. Here's a pillow primer to help guide your choices:

Boudoir: This 12- by 16-inch pillow is used decoratively but also creates a nice resting spot for your head when placed on top of a sleeping pillow and propped up against the headboard.

European: Two or three of these 26- by 26-inch squares can stand in as a headboard on a bed without one and also make a comfortable place to rest your back when reading in bed. They make a pretty background for smaller pillows placed in front of them.

King: King-size beds are often dressed with two of these 26- by 36-inch rectangles. Some people don't find them comfortable for sleeping, so they are often fitted with pretty shams to serve a decorative purpose. One king pillow on a double or twin bed makes a nice backdrop for smaller pillows placed in front.

Neck roll: The standard length and diameter of these tubular pillows is 16 by 6 inches, but I have seen bed-width versions that make a dramatic statement when placed in front of a headboard, with or without two standard pillows placed in front. The smaller, more typical size can be used, as the name suggests, for neck support while sitting up in bed.

Queen: These pillows, which are 26 by 30 inches, are generally harder to find than standard- or king-size bed pillows. If you like a more substantial pillow than a standard size but not one as massive as a king, it is worth searching for a queen version.

Russian: This 14- by 14-inch square is decorative, especially when set in front of European pillows (which lean against the headboard) and a neck roll placed in front. The look is symmetrical and neat—a good choice for a man's bedroom, perhaps. (Standard bed pillows can lay flat and out of view under the European shams.)

Standard: The most common and, some say, the most comfortable for sleeping, this 20- by 26-inch pillow is perfect for snuggling into for a night's rest or a daytime nap.

Travel: This 20- by 15-inch pillow can be decorative and practical: You can roll it up and tie it into a small neck roll.

Children's Rooms

While there is so much furniture available for children of all ages—and some pieces are fun—I recommend choosing furniture that is more classic and long-lasting. I like the value of good things. You can put a bunk bed in the room and apply glow-in-the-dark stars to the ceiling, and that's okay . . . temporarily. But eventually a child outgrows these youthful furnishings. People hesitate to spend a lot of money on children's furniture, but I say you can teach children so much about value, pride of ownership, and even some history when you choose high-quality classic furnishings. A beautiful dresser or bed frame can stay with a child forever and perhaps be reinvented as something else in the future. A youngster's twin bed can become an elegant daybed just by changing the linens and pillows. She can use the dresser in her own home someday, in a bedroom or anywhere a beautiful chest of drawers is useful. Fine furniture is a family heirloom, so you can also look forward to your children passing down quality furnishings to their own children, and so on down the line.

As for décor, I love poster beds and light-colored textiles for girls and somewhat darker woods and graphic color schemes, like blue or black and cream, for boys. I always used strong silhouettes in my son's room when he was growing up. Even though you are making an investment and playing a part in the selection process, you can still respect and develop children's thoughts and feelings. For example, if you know your daughter loves lilacs, you can put them all around the room or use them in the fabric. If your son loves cars, his collection can be kept on a beautiful cherry desk or on oak bookshelves. Later, he can use the desk and bookshelves when

he moves to take his first job. If the pieces are classic and strong, they will always be useful. As ever, romantic decorating is about quality, comfort, and luxury, and that's just as important in a child's bedroom as in your living room. Creating a cozy retreat complete with warm, personal touches and classic pieces gives your little ones a soothing atmosphere and room to grow.

✳ ABOVE: *A dresser like this is perfect for a girl's or teen's bedroom, but it's classic and well enough made to last her all her life. When your young lady grows up, she can use the pieces in any room; for example, the mirror can be used in a living room, and the dresser can hold silverware in a dining room.*

Guest Rooms

I don't have a lot of guests (just family mostly), but when they do come to stay, I want them to be comfortable. The beds in my guest rooms are very plush and adorned with lace coverings and lots of soft pillows. I like to drape the windows with yards of either linen or silk, often tea-dyed to complement the pale tones of the walls and floors. This gives a room a serene feeling, perfect for sleeping and resting. Above all else, you want to make your guests feel at ease and wanted when they're away from home. If you rarely entertain overnight guests, you may want your guest room to do double duty as a craft room or a home office.

In that case, a desk and a chair are a must, along with wicker or fabric-covered boxes to store needed supplies in style.

My guest room on the second level has an even more elaborately carved French bed than the one in my room. It's dressed in crisp and inviting white cotton and lace bedding. Diane Burn designed the baldachin above the bed, using

❋ BELOW: *This guest room is done in very soft peachy beige tones. The heavily carved French bed is an antique.*

❋ OPPOSITE: *Like more vintage armoires, this one is too shallow to hold (and hide) a television. Instead, guests can place clothes and personal belongings inside, on its shelves, since the room does not have a dresser.*

fabric from my own factory. The round table near the window is topped with pale fabric and a white tablecloth that is enhanced with open work and embroidery. A chaise is positioned to enjoy views out the window. The tables in the room have revolving collections—sometimes boxes, sometimes statuary. My brother, Jack, recently bought me an Art Deco–era pincushion (it's his favorite design period) with a figure of a pretty lady on top, and I keep that in the guest room. As always, fresh flowers bring some cheer to the setting. The home's only original fireplace is also flanked with two very old, comfortable French chairs. The armoire in the room is my favorite one in the house. The carving is really extraordinary, and the tone of the bleached wood is so perfect.

The wall treatment is interesting in this room. It's paneled almost up to the ceiling and was installed as a way of incorporating the trumeau mirror over the fireplace. The paneling gives the room a cozy quality. The wow factor comes from how high the paneling goes, and it's very doable at home. The paint treatment is called *strie* (pronounced stree-*ay*). To create the look, drag a straight, wide long-haired brush through wet glaze to form fine, thin vertical lines. It almost has the appearance of natural wood. The color is the softest, warmest peach. Everyone who sleeps in this room says they have a restful night.

There are more guest quarters on the third level of the house. One room has a painted bed with a canopy above. It is a beautiful three-sided box embellished with molding and carving and painted in a lively combination of soft greens and gold. A carpenter or someone who is confident about their woodworking skills could easily replicate this with some plywood, beautiful

VENICE LACE

This is a heavily embroidered silken lace with an all-over repeated pattern. It is often used as an appliqué on garments but can also be used as a table topper and pillow covering when placed over a solid fabric such as silk or taffeta.

trim moldings, and medallions. To create a really grand and romantic look, attach the canopy at the top of the wall. The fabric can be installed on all three sides with Velcro, staples, or upholstery tacks. To achieve the rich folds, buy fabric that is three times the depth and width of the sides and back of the canopy and long enough to hit the floor after hemming. The bed is dressed in a frothy mixture of white linen and lace bedspread and pillows. It's hard to resist taking a nap in all that soft comfort.

Another guest room is very small. (I call it "the baby's room.") It's the kind of diminutive, extra bedroom that exists in a lot of homes—but I still managed to address all the comforts an overnight guest might desire. The double bed is awash in soft laces. The canopy is quite large. I love the scale of it, especially in the small room. It works because the color scheme is monochromatic and pale. It would not work as well if the canopy was brightly colored or dark; it would overwhelm the room. Two matching French side tables, a small arm chair, simple bookshelves tucked into a nook big enough to hold a small television, and some favorite reading material complete the room. A closet holds hanging clothes and boxes. The single window is dressed with silk drapes. What more do you need, really?

✳ LEFT: *This pretty pincushion, a gift from my brother, adds character to the guest room. It's personal and pretty— whimsical, too!*

✳ BELOW: *The carving on this guest room bed is very unique; however, I have seen reproduction head- and footboards with details that are just as pretty and much more affordable than this expensive, imported antique.*

✳ OPPOSITE: *A bench like this is a welcome addition to any bedroom. It's a convenient place to sit while removing slippers or shoes, and it's a nice perch for an overnight bag or a tray filled with tea and cookies.*

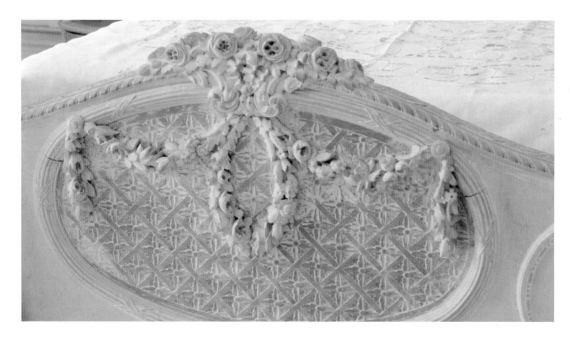

Bathroom Retreats

My bathroom is truly a romantic retreat. I purposely designed it to be a magical place where all the cares of the day can be washed away and I can be renewed. That's the way all bathrooms should be. Why settle for a sterile space with no character just because it's a bathroom? You can create an elegant, relaxing feeling in any master bathroom or powder room if you pay attention to the finishes and storage. For instance, walls can be painted in a soft peach or rose, which is very flattering to skin tone. Tumbled or polished marble, or stone-look ceramic tile, in shades of pink, buttery cream, or taupe on the floor is practical and has Old World charm.

You needn't sacrifice fashion for function. Clutter control can be accomplished with romantic flair! Etched- or frosted-glass containers can hold everything from cotton balls to makeup brushes. And French milled soaps piled in a silver bowl make a design statement while still keeping needed bars close at hand. Lots of fluffy towels stacked on a towel rack or neatly folded over gleaming brass or nickel towel bars add even more luxury. A soft, fluffy terry-cloth robe (maybe with your monogram embroidered on its breast) hung on a substantial hook is very welcoming. So you see, it's not that difficult to make even a tiny bathroom special.

Taking a bath is quintessentially romantic and restful, so try to make the time for it. My tub is unique—it is actually two Victorian tubs that were cut in half and joined together for symmetry. Most Victorian tubs were high on one end and sloped down lower on the other. I wanted a tub that was even on both ends. The tub was reenameled, so the seam is invisible. The cast-iron shell was then encased in a custom-made

Battenberg Lace

A bold Renaissance lace made with thick cotton embroidery and cutwork technique, this lace is usually trimmed with sequins, crystal beads, or pearls.

carved stone envelope. The faucet is in the shape of a swan, adding further romance and fantasy to the tub area. Of course, creating a custom bathtub is not practical for most people. But you can make your bathtub area (even if it's a molded

fiberglass model from the local home store) soft and inviting with the addition of some pillar candles and a small cream-colored chair or footstool repurposed as a mini table to hold soap and a sea sponge, a towel, or a book and a glass of bubbly.

There is always a pretty chair draped with an interesting piece of lace and a beautiful table next to the tub. Sometimes I use a set of mirrored nesting tables, and other times I place a small wooden oval or glass-topped table nearby. If you can fit a small table next to your tub, it's a good place to set a cup or glass and a book or magazine. That's what I do when I really want to relax. I don't take a bath as often as I would like (I am in and out of the shower every morning), but I do try to indulge in a restorative soak at least once a month. I always place a bowl or vase of flowers on the table, and I have a little glass of wine. I must

have a beautiful robe draped over a chair so I can slip into it and wrap myself up when I am done. With some classical music playing, it just feels wonderful. An hour later, I am out and feeling rested. I put on silk pajamas and a robe and have a light dinner. We all deserve to enjoy life's little luxuries, especially when we're convinced there simply isn't time in the day. There's always time to be good to yourself.

✻ ABOVE, LEFT: *The details are what make my bathroom special. The cherub statue could just as easily find a home in the garden, but I like it next to my tub.*
✻ ABOVE, RIGHT: *The painted floor makes me smile. What a nice way to start the day!*
✻ OPPOSITE: *This large armoire is a showstopper. It was originally used in a lady's shop in Paris. Now it holds clothing, linens, and toiletries.*

Aside from the dramatic tub, my favorite part of the bathroom is the floor, which sounds funny, I know. The decorative artist Amy McGill painted the most beautiful angels (called *putti*), ribbons, and flowers on it. A large, white glass chandelier lights up the room, and diaphanous lace curtains maintain a sense of privacy while still letting a lot of sunshine into the room. A specially made arched-pine and etched-glass door encloses the shower. This is an idea that can definitely be translated into a standard shower stall. A carpenter or bathroom designer can help you work out the details of framing a shower-stall door with a sealed wood frame. Or consider revamping a plain shower door with the addition of an etched-glass panel (available at home superstores and kitchen and bath design shops).

An old painted Victorian mantelpiece, in what is a very original use, serves as an elaborate backsplash for the pedestal sink. Again, this idea can be replicated in any home with a large bathroom. I frequently spot vintage fireplace mantels in antique stores. There is no reason that a handyperson or carpenter could not attach one to a wall (making the appropriate openings for plumbing) and then install a pedestal or wall sink below. I added wicker baskets on both sides of the mantel to hold hand towels and other bathroom necessities, taking the place of a more expected medicine cabinet. The mirror above the

❋ OPPOSITE: *I used an antique painted fireplace mantel and mirror to serve as a backdrop to the vintage pedestal sink. Baskets attached to either side are both pretty and practical storage.*

❋ RIGHT, TOP: *Antique lace is a pretty decoration hanging from a hook.*

❋ RIGHT, BOTTOM: *My shower closet features etched glass, mirrors, and a "rainfall" fixture.*

mantel is attached directly to the wall, and it is graced by exuberant leaf carvings. Two pretty ribbon-and-bow sconces, similar to the ones in my bedroom, flank the mantel. A simple wicker wastebasket and two chairs complete the sink area. You can see why I love my bathroom so much!

The centerpiece in the room is a large vanity table that a carpenter made for me out of plywood in a classic long, oval shape. Tables like this one, though not quite as long, are easy to find at secondhand stores, since they were so popular for the first fifty years of the last century. Or you can have one made inexpensively to your exact size specifications. A dressing table is such a bonus in a bathroom or bedroom. I picture a model or an actress sitting there and using it to apply makeup and perfume. You can do that, too. Cover yours,

as I do mine, with linen and lace. I first covered the table with some inexpensive quilt padding (available by the yard in fabric stores; you can also use felt). Then I placed three layers of fabric, which I change fairly regularly. A boudoir chair with a carved frame and a caned seat, back, and sides makes a perfect perch.

I collect perfume bottles, and this is where I display them, along with fresh flowers (of course), a pretty table mirror, and a terra-cotta bust of a young girl. Perfume bottles are fun to find. I look for them when I travel and in local San Francisco antique stores. There are also good copies of old pieces available in gift and home-design stores; you can collect those if the original versions are hard to find or too expensive. They are just as lovely. Crystal jars and bottles, candlesticks, and powder boxes complete the table. Arranging items on a table like this is easy if you keep the items in a similar style and group like things together—perfume bottles together in one spot, glass jars in another. Tall items, like the bust or the vase of flowers, look best when placed off to the side and toward the back.

An oversize bleached pine armoire is a regal addition to the vanity room. It has a full-length oval mirror on the front and is crowned by wreath, swag, and elaborate crosshatch carving. Glass side cabinets filled with shelves for storing knits and scarves make clothing into a beautiful display. A large tassel makes opening the doors easy. It's details like these that give the piece individuality. If you have room for it, adding a beautifully detailed freestanding storage piece to a bathroom, even a small chest of drawers or a bookshelf, is very romantic and practical, since you can use it to hold soap, towels, shampoo, and other bath-related items.

Guest Bathrooms

Guest bathrooms should also be comfortable and elegant, even if they are small. Mine is a long, narrow bathroom done in blue and white tile. I love the crispness of that design. It looks very clean and neat. And the old-fashioned Victorian-style toilet with pull chain, which I put in, always prompts interest, curiosity, and a smile. Who says you can't learn a little about the past when washing your hands?

An oval pedestal sink with ample room on both sides for toiletries is new but based on a vintage style. The antique mirror on the wall adds even more charm to the room. Why use a standard medicine cabinet when there are so many interesting mirrors, both new and old, on the market? On the opposite wall, I placed a more typical old cupboard with tiny shelves for all the potions and lotions a guest could possibly need. Never forget to stock the guest bath with fresh towels.

The shower stall is comfortably ample and has a standard glass door. I actually love this shower and use it more than the one in my bathroom. For romantic drama and to show my guests I care, the shower entrance is framed with a long drape of white embroidered cotton pulled through two rings on each side of the shower stall and one in the ceiling. This is a simple project anyone can accomplish (see page 186 for shower swag how-to). The swag ring and hooks are gold-toned but have tarnished with time, which is so much prettier than when they were bright and shiny.

A small powder room off the entryway is a convenient place for guests to freshen up when they come to call. A small, original stained-glass window maintains privacy. The fixtures are gold-toned and include a toilet-paper cover, triple hand-towel rods, and a vintage-style soap dish. Since I use a sweetly scented liquid soap here, because it's neater and more hygienic than bar soap, I use the soap dish as a place to keep perfume bottles. I lined it with a pretty piece of lace first. When ladies come to call, they can spritz themselves with either one of these pleasant scents.

A note on fragrance at home: A romantic home engages all the senses—lovely things to look at, delicious food to eat, wonderful music, and pleasing scents. I am not one for scented candles, heavy perfume, or intense potpourri. However, the smell of a clean house or a light floral or citrus scent in the air from a spritz of good perfume is pleasant. Fragrances should be clean (not heavy or sweet) and kept as subtle notes in the background.

✳ OPPOSITE: *Give your girlfriends a treat by placing your favorite fragrance in the powder room within easy reach.*

✳ ABOVE, LEFT: *A fairly standard shower is transformed into a space fit for royalty with just a few yards of flowery netting. Lace in a variety of colors, patterns, and textures can be purchased by the yard at most large fabric stores. All you need to complete this simple decorating project is a few cup hooks and two tassels or pretty ribbon.*

✳ ABOVE, RIGHT: *The lace is simply attached to the wall with a brass cup hook and a small tassel.*

✳ LEFT: *This old-fashioned toilet isn't vintage; it is a reproduction, even though it looks original to the house. There are so many different kinds of bathroom fixtures available today that you can have an antique look without sacrificing modern technology and function.*

Chapter Six

In-Between Spaces and Hidden Rooms

A house is so much more than a group of rooms. Hallways and staircases connect them, and small nooks and secret spaces contribute to the overall ambience of a romantic home. And why shouldn't every corner of a house, even those that are simply passed through or unseen by most visitors, be filled with beauty and charm?

The Entryway

The original entryway of my house was closed off from the main hallway and was covered in dark paneling and old, dark wooden flooring, which was not particularly special. I changed all that. I changed the doors as well; the old doors were dark and forbidding wood. I had double glass and iron doors made to fit the space. The iron is finished in a pale green, and there is a lot of movement in the swirls and vines that make up the pattern. Changing a solid door to one with glass inserts is an excellent way to visually lighten and open up a small, dark entryway that cannot be enlarged.

I removed the walls in the entryway and made it one big open space, covered the floor in a bright, light marble inlay pattern (similar to the one in my dining room), and painted the walls a beautiful cream. Now when you come in, you can see all the way to the back of the house and into the garden. It's so light and airy. If there is anything you can do to open up the main entry of your house, consider it. It makes such a difference not only to your family and guests, but also to you. When I step into the entry, I am immediately transported to a relaxing place. A dark, cramped entry would certainly have the opposite effect on my mood.

✳ ABOVE: *The portico and iron doors make entering the house all the more dramatic.*

✳ OPPOSITE: *I am fortunate to have such a large entryway. It's a comfortable place for guests to take off their hats and coats. The unique humpbacked settees are perfect for sitting down to remove shoes.*

THE STAIRCASE

The staircase in my house is to the left of the entry as you come in. Originally, it had a plain wooden railing and stairs. There was nothing exciting about it. I really wanted to express a French or European idea, so I replaced the wooden railing with an iron one in the same finish and pattern as the front doors. Iron stair rails were popular during the Regency period and the early 19th century—and feel very French to me. What a difference it makes; the ironwork is so lacy that the staircase feels open. Anyone with a plain staircase railing can use this idea. Ready-made iron railings in a number of undulating patterns are available. If you cannot find something you like, you can always have one custom made.

A huge, dark stained-glass window originally loomed on the wall above the first stair landing. It did not let any light in, so I had the colored glass replaced with clear and frosted pieces. The large center pane of glass was an image of brown cattails and murky water, as I recall. It was something very Victorian, to say the least. I had it replaced with the etched glass you see there now. It was a big job but so worth the effort and time, because that large window has brightened the entire area.

The mural going up the wall is very special. The girl in the picture is one of my models. The scene is my romantic vision. Notice that the gazebo has a frieze of sewing details, such as a needle and thread and a scissors. It's a personal statement, incorporated almost secretly right into the painting. When the mural was originally painted, it was too bright and realistic looking. It was as if the scene was really there. That is not the look I wanted, so I asked the artist, Roxana Santos de Hayden, to soften it with a glaze. Several coats

WROUGHT AND CAST IRON

Wrought iron is pounded out with hammers, a labor-intensive process. Cast iron, on the other hand, is formed by pouring molten iron into a mold. Wrought iron is stronger than cast iron, but cast iron is easier and less expensive to produce.

✳ ABOVE: *The ironwork was custom-made for the staircase. It's very French in feeling.*

✳ ABOVE: *A stairway wall, so often neglected, is a perfect place for a mural, either hand-painted like mine or a wallpaper version.*

of glaze (and some frustration on her part) later, it was perfect. My idea was to have the image be extremely subtle, like a dream. And that's what she accomplished.

If you are put off by the prospect of painting a mural up the staircase yourself, there are so many talented decorative painters in every city and town, you can probably find one you like to do the job. Make sure to visit some of their previous work before making a decision, so you are confident you like their style. Wallpaper murals are also available. If they are too bright or defined, they can be softened with a soft wash of white glaze over the top of it. Be sure to practice on a spare piece of wallpaper first to perfect the look you're after.

✳ ABOVE, LEFT: *The staircase details make it so dramatic.*
✳ ABOVE, RIGHT: *Coppola's cutting room—not exactly a room anymore, but certainly filled with romance, mystery—and extra china!*

THE CUTTING ROOM

In the beginning of this book, I talked about the romance of a home's history. My house is certainly filled with history. Some people say there's even a friendly female ghost in the house, although I have never seen her. There's another interesting hidden space in the house, however, that holds a lot of cinematic history, and that is the darkroom. This is the room where Francis Ford Coppola edited the *Godfather* movies and his last movie as owner of the house, *Apocalypse Now*. It's a simple, quirky room, a large closet really, now used for storage but kept intact. There is no decoration to speak of in the room, but the idea of such a space is very romantic. It's one of the elements that give the house its character. If you live in an old house, you know what I mean. There is always a little room or space off in a corner or in an attic somewhere that is quirky and funny and that you don't want to touch. It just adds to the ambience and energy of the house.

THE WINE CELLAR

I keep my wine in a specially designed cellar, which is in the basement of the house and accessed from the back stairs. The space had already been designed to house wine when I bought the house, and I find it very useful. I am not a collector, but I had a close friend who was, and these wines represent his interests. It's certainly romantic to have a wine cellar and collect bottles to save and store there. You learn so much about wine regions and winemakers. So if you are interested in wine, indulge your passion. Many people turn small areas of their basements into storage for spirits. In my cellar, simple painted wooden shelves in a diamond formation keep the bottles at just the right angle for storage and occasional turning. Plain tags with handwritten identification make finding just the right wine a snap. Conventional wooden shelves are attached to the facing walls, and this is where hard spirits are kept, as bottles of good Scotch and vodka should be stored upright, not on their sides. The room is

set at 55°F and maintains a level of at least 50 percent humidity, which my expert friends tell me is the perfect environment for storing liquors and wines, also ensuring that the corks don't dry out and ruin the wines.

Decanting Fine Wine

Pouring wine out of its bottle into a clear glass decanter does three things: It eliminates sediment from older wines, aerates the wine so it tastes better, and allows you and your friends to enjoy the color of the wine. Most young wines do not have to be decanted, but it's fun, especially if you have three or four people to enjoy it with at one sitting. When decanting an older wine that has sediment (hold the bottle up to the light and you will see it), Arthur recommends pouring very slowly and stopping as soon as you see sediment in the bottle's neck. Let the decanted red wine sit for about twenty to thirty minutes before serving. White wine can also be decanted, but it need not sit for more than five or ten minutes before pouring.

THE ATELIER

If I had to say there was one place where I did real at-home work, it would be the atelier off my bedroom. If you have a home office or a work area, make it as beautiful as the rest of your house so you want to spend time there. There's no reason to use drab office furniture for a workspace, especially one in your home! In my case, once the bathroom was done, architect Diane Burns and I decided the remaining space would make a good storage and home office space. She designed a series of built-in floor-to-ceiling closets against one wall. (Victorians did not have any closets, so the house is sorely lacking in them.) I keep off-season clothes there, among other things. Anytime you can add built-in storage, you should do it, because it is so useful. The inside panels of the pale green closet doors were stenciled in a creamy pattern that reminds me of lattice- or fretwork.

I added an antique French slant-front desk to the long, narrow room. It's small and perfect for me. On it, I keep a phone, a writing pad, a calendar, and the books that I am currently reading. The desk is dark wood, mahogany most likely. I don't mind a piece of dark furniture to offset a muted color palette and provide a bit of contrast. Someone asked me recently why I put a piece of dark furniture in my house, and I said, "I do what I like." In this case, it's a small desk that's right for the space. That's an important principle to keep in mind when decorating or designing a room. You don't have to be so rigid that you can't bring yourself to introduce something a little different into a scheme, especially when the piece might be appropriate.

An antique dress form, given to me on my birthday a few years ago, is both a whimsical dec-

orative accent and a practical one, too. Sometimes I rush out of the office with a fabric I am working with, and I have to bring it home with me. So when I get upstairs, I place it on the form to see

BONHEUR DU JOUR

A desk developed toward the end of the 18th century and designed specifically for use by a lady for writing letters in her boudoir.

how it drapes on a body and catches the light. I will be inspired by fabric and make different shapes to see if I am pleased. It can't be used for its original purpose, but it does make a nice place for fabric. And then I may sit and sketch for a while.

A large crystal and brass chandelier hangs overhead, providing a lot of sparkle and light. However, the room does have floor-to-ceiling windows, which are covered with silk balloon shades that diffuse the natural light. The fabric has a hint of green in the weft to coordinate with the color on the walls and closet doors. Covered baskets in the corner provide discreet storage for items I want to keep at hand but don't want to look at all the time.

My atelier is a feminine space. However, when creating a home office for a man, bring in some leather, perhaps in the form of strong pieces of classically shaped furniture. I love old French club chairs to lounge and read in, especially when the leather is distressed and dark with age. They contrast well with a muted palette, so you don't have to go the route of traditional forest green or cranberry walls for a den. A lamp to read by and shelves filled with interesting personal things would make any man happy. I love toile for men, too. I would use it in black and white to lend a masculine feeling to the room. Choose black or navy accessories for a man's den, such as lamps and lampshades, and perhaps a throw. Black defines silhouettes and makes a masculine statement.

Daydreamy Corners

There are a few rooms on the top level of my house that are perfect for daydreaming, enjoying the view of the Golden Gate Bridge and San Francisco Bay, or maybe just taking a nap. A daybed fitted with a white slipcover sits by a large window in the corner of one of the upper rooms. Lots of pillows make it a nice place to curl up with a book. If you have an extra room, a daybed is a practical, pretty way to furnish it. A guest can stay overnight, and it doubles as a sofa or a chaise during the day.

There is a distinctive three-part chaise in a second top-floor room, which can be configured for lounging or for a tête-à-tête with a friend. Having an out-of-the-way spot to go to when you want to get away from the hustle and bustle is such a pleasure, and this corner is set up for just such occasions. If you don't have a spare room to devote to quiet time, carve an intimate space out of a larger living room or master suite by placing a chaise in an out-of-the-way corner, preferably near a window or fireplace. Soft pillows, a cozy throw, a side table to hold a drink, and a good book are all you need to create your own little Versailles. How romantic!

A three-panel screen strategically placed is an even better way of making a private "room" for yourself in a large space like a great room or family room. And it's movable, so you can put it anywhere you need a little intimacy or drama. Simply fold it up and store it under a bed or in a closet when not in use.

Couch

The term used to describe a daybed in the 17th and 18th centuries; the word was not adopted as a common synonym for sofa until the early 20th century.

Chapter Seven

NATURE PERFECTED: GARDEN ROOMS AND GARDENS

Gardens are restful places. I love to play with the dogs or just sit and think or read in mine. When I am dining alone, I often eat in the garden room and look out at the pool that sits in the center of the Italian-inspired courtyard. It's very relaxing. Nature is good for the soul. Whether you have acres of property in the country or just a few window boxes separating your apartment from the cityscape, green spaces are such an important aspect of the romantic home.

THE GARDEN ROOM

The garden room is my sanctuary. It's a small space surrounded almost entirely by glass, giving it the feel of a conservatory. Floor-to-ceiling Palladium windows open up three sides to the outdoors and give it a spacious feel, blurring the boundaries between the indoor and outdoor world. I also invite the garden inside by filling the intimate space with flowering plants, foliage, and a ficus tree. You can transform an ordinary sunroom into a romantic setting with beautiful furnishings inspired by nature, potted plants, and garden statuary.

A small round table, covered with crocheted lace over a full-length jacquard tablecloth in a pale green, softens the marble floor in my garden room. If you can cover your sunroom with a stone floor, such as marble or slate, you can pot and water plants without worry. The chairs have a slight green tinge (see page 202 for information on creating a painted finish inspired by these chairs). A painted white sideboard holds

CONSERVATORY

A conservatory is a structure made primarily of glass and attached to a house. In the 18th and 19th centuries, collecting exotic plants and growing flowers and fruits out of season was a popular pastime; and conservatories, which could be quite elaborate, grew in popularity.

pads and pencils (in case design inspiration strikes) and a small television, perfect for catching up on the news.

I fell in love with the lacelike quality of the metal fruit stand that now sits near the table. A marble-topped wrought console table holds books and accessories, but it could just as easily be used as a potting table. Venetian glass wall sconces are

delicate and lacelike, too, and their floral motif is in keeping with the room's subtle theme. Plants abound and change frequently according to the season. I love to display orchids in the garden room, but I also have bowls and urns filled with variegated ivy and tropical foliage—all of which are available at nurseries and home centers.

Wicker furniture painted a creamy white or pale green is a casual yet graceful choice for a traditional romantic garden room. Cushions and pillows made from ticking or linen add crispness and comfort. Iron garden furniture, especially pieces featuring floral motifs, is also very pretty and practical in a sunroom. Of course, if your garden room is well protected from the elements, you can also choose to decorate with standard interior furnishings, as I have done in mine. I like the flexibility of being able to mix and match furnishings from other rooms in the house. And why shouldn't a garden room have the same warmth and sophistication as a living room or bedroom?

The showstopping element in the room is a large carved arch from Asia. It is filled with intricate carvings of birds and flowers—perfect for a garden room. The distressed whitewashed finish is rustic and contrasts nicely with the more refined elements in the room. The Chinese writing carved into it stands for success. It also shows that you can mix some Asian elements into a traditional or romantic home, and it works if the palette and scale are in step. I also like the idea of using fragments from old buildings and structures to add architectural character to a room. You can find decorative architectural details similar to my Asian arch in salvage yards and at flea markets.

THE GARDEN

My small backyard garden is a wonderland. It is my interpretation of a classic Italianate garden, which relies on three basic elements—evergreens, stonework, and water—and a design philosophy based on order and geometry. The Italian-inspired approach is a practical and low-maintenance one that works well for small urban gardens. If you are apartment-bound, plant a miniature garden in an urn or a wide, shallow bowl and place it on a table or deep windowsill. If you're working with a sprawling suburban yard, it's romantic to carve out small areas or outside rooms by having a stone patio installed and perhaps even a small pool or fountain, so you can create intimate, personalized living spaces even in the great outdoors.

Once the basic structure of the garden is in place, you can add statues, urns, and pots filled with simple flowers. When planning a patio garden, consider how it will be seen from the inside. If it is possible to create a small garden and seating area adjacent to your dining or living room, do so. You get double the pleasure from a garden you can see and enjoy from indoors. My garden is visible from the dining room; it's so nice to gaze at the pool and the foliage during a dinner party.

My garden is basically symmetrical, which gives it a formal feel. I had a raised patio built off of the garden room and dining room that runs the full width of the back of the house. You step down onto a stone-covered area that is surrounded by planting beds. In the middle is a small reflecting pool. It has three curves, like a clover. When Francis Ford Coppola lived in the house, he would entertain in the garden, and his friends must have dangled their feet in the water. I must admit, I do not go into the pool, although

when my dogs were younger, they liked splashing around in it. I do love looking at it in the evening or when the sun is setting. The still, flat surface of the water reflects a perfect mirror image of the garden, the sky, and the moonlight.

Four urns decorate the edge of the pool. Each is filled with an ever-changing mix of white and pink flowers. They spill over the edges of the containers, softening the hard borders with untamed abandon. Other urns dotting the stone patio are filled with evergreens (boxwood, holly, and yew are good choices because they can be clipped into topiaries and are easy to grow in most climates) and lavender. The beds are filled with annual color from impatiens and petunias and from perennials such as lavender and, of course, roses in shades of white, pink, and purple. Camel-

lia bushes are planted along the right side of the backyard. Depending on your climate and soil situation, hydrangeas, peonies, heather, white and pink yarrow, and pink, white, or purple phlox also make romantic additions to the garden. They also smell wonderful. The light floral scent of a summer garden drifting through open windows and into your home is intoxicating.

Three large streetlights are strategically placed around the perimeter of the garden. They were installed while Coppola lived in the house and were, in fact, used in *The Godfather* movies—another piece of cinema history right in my backyard. They still work and light the area with a warm glow, highlighting plants and other garden features at night. Why not use a vintage city streetlight in your garden? It's both practical and

charming. Such items can be found at salvage yards, and any electrician can rewire them for safe use. Reproduction streetlights are also available at home centers. They add a bit of dash and style to the garden.

Notice that I have not named any rare or specialty flowers or plants. I am not a plantswoman, and I don't have a lot of time to devote to tracking down unusual specimens that require special care (although a gardener helps me maintain what I grow). A garden can be just as romantic with plants you find at the local nursery as long you choose a variety of textures and a soft color palette. I love lavenders and fuchsias—and of course white offers softness. I use very little yellow. I don't think it's as romantic a color, unless you put it with lace. But if you like soft yellows, express yourself and use it in your garden and your home! The vines, trailing plants, evergreens,

(continued on page 154)

✳ OPPOSITE, LEFT: *The streetlights are real; they were used in* The Godfather *movies!*

✳ OPPOSITE, RIGHT: *The garden as it looked when the house was built and, later on, in the 1950s.*

✳ ABOVE: *The reflecting pool was created when Francis Ford Coppola owned the house. It's fun to think about the parties he must have had in the garden—his guests dipping their toes in the water on warm evenings. The large concrete containers are always overflowing with flowers.*

ROMANTIC VINES AND TRAILING PLANTS

As they climb a trellis, meander along a wall, or spill out of a pot, vines and trailing plants add lush and sinuous texture to a garden. So many are easy to care for and provide green structure and background to a garden, much like foundation plants or shrubbery but in a more exuberant fashion. A romantic bonus: Many flowering vines and trailers attract hummingbirds and butterflies. Here are some of my favorite vines. Plant them along a plain fence, arrange them in a tall planter or a hanging pot, train them on a trellis or arbor, or use them as ground cover. Ask your nursery specialist or consult a good gardening book for planting how-to and care in your climate. I have used common names, so you may recognize many of them.

Vines

Cardinal climber: **The foliage and flowers of this vine are similar to those of the cypress vine—and hummingbirds can't resist its nectar.**

Clematis: **This perennial vine blooms in early spring through late summer and sometimes again in the fall. Its flowers can range in size from small (1 inch across) to large (4 inches across) and come in a variety of whites, pinks, and purples. It climbs using tendrils, which wrap around almost any structure, including a stone wall or a wooden fence, arbor, or latticework.**

Cypress vine: **This climber has fine feathery foliage and small, red tubular flowers. It's good for partly shady gardens and will grow 10 to 20 feet. Hummingbirds love it.**

English ivy: **A classic sturdy vine that provides a shiny green backdrop for other plants and garden furnishings. It's a fast grower but can be controlled by cutting it back yearly when it threatens to encroach on neighboring plants. I trained and trimmed mine to surround the mirrors in my back courtyard.**

Japanese honeysuckle: **This fast-growing vine produces numerous tubular-shaped white and cream-colored flowers that have a sweet scent, which** means it is attractive to hummingbirds and butterflies. The scent is especially noticeable on summer evenings. This vine will cover a fence, wall, or trellis in just a few years.

Moonflower: **Moonflower has huge (6 to 8 inches) fragrant white flowers that open after sunset to bask in the glorious moonlight—the ultimate romantic vine!**

Morning glory: **This is an annual that acts like a perennial because it self-sows its seeds without restraint. Flowers come in white, pink, red, violet, and the classic sky blue. The flowers open during morning hours and sometimes again in the evening.**

Sweet pea: **This is an annual climber that should be planted by seed instead of started plants, so that the sprouts grow up a trellis in the spring. The flowers smell so sweet and look so pretty in a vase. Flowers come in a variety of colors, including pale reds, pinks, blue, violet, coral, cream, and bright white.**

Sweet potato vine: **This vine comes in a variety of colors, from very dark purple, called "Blackie," to the bright chartreuse of "Margarita," and even a "Tri-Color" version that has white, green, and pink leaves—how pretty! Sweet potato vines do well in hanging containers, in urns, and as a ground cover.**

Wisteria: This fast-growing, sturdy vine sports lavender-colored flower brackets that are synonymous with Victorian gardens. Expect to wait a few years before the plant starts to flower. For the best results, make sure that its roots are planted in rich organic matter and set in the shade and that the top vines reach the sun.

Trailing Plants

Alyssum: Dense clusters of tiny, round snow-white flowers characterize this compact, mounding trailer. The flowers bloom continuously throughout the growing season in a seemingly endless parade. They create a polka-dot effect that I love.

Candytuft: This sturdy perennial looks delicate and lacy. It's a low, frilly plant that produces mounds of beautiful, round ice-white, pink, or lilac flowers that last for several months.

Ferns: There are many species of ferns, and several look pretty in hanging baskets and pots, even indoors. Their fronds cascade nicely. I placed three large hanging baskets full of faux ferns in a large pine tree at the back of the garden to hide an adjacent apartment building. They do a good job of it, and everyone thinks they are real.

Verbena: Clusters of red, rose, peach, pink, purple, lavender, or blue round flowers rise above dark green wrinkly or toothed leaves.

Vinca (also known as myrtle, creeping myrtle, or periwinkle): This is a short evergreen perennial ground cover with small, round purple flowers that come and go each spring, leaving behind a soft trailing habit of dark, shiny green leaves.

Wave petunias: This is a hybrid version of the common annual petunia. Its numerous blooms come in a range of colors, including red, pink, white, and purple. It's so easy to grow and looks beautiful when combined with candytuft or alyssum. It's very romantic when placed in a window box on a balcony, so the flowers can spill over the edge.

and annual color should all work together to create an uninterrupted backdrop—a neutral canvas upon which you can "paint" with furnishings and garden accessories.

I enjoy decorating with mirrors in the garden as well. I once saw a garden that featured mirrors arranged to create reflections of reflections. Like an infinity pool, it appeared to go on and on forever. I knew I had to have that effect in my own outdoor space. This is a good example of what I meant when I talked earlier about being inspired by what you see.

Mirrors help expand a small outdoor area, and they reflect the pool and the plants. Mine are arched, just like many of the mirrors inside my house, and clipped ivy surrounds them to create a natural frame. Visitors always think I have an endless garden because of the mirrors. If you like the idea of adding mirrors to your garden but live in a colder climate and worry about the glass becoming damaged, simply take the mirrors inside during the winter months (although nothing has ever happened to my mirrors, and it does get cold and rainy in San Francisco). Actually, the elements naturally age the mirrors, adding further to their historical allure and distressed elegance.

Since my house is detached, I have two narrow side gardens. Evergreen hedges line one avenue, along with an assortment of mossy statuary. It's like an Italian grotto, shaded from the sun and

very cool even when it's hot outside. A trellis rose garden that provides me with fragrant cuttings all summer long lines the other side. The trellis is covered with arched latticework and Plexiglas. I had indoor hanging lights installed along the pathway that the trellis and arbor create. The Plexiglas protects them from the elements, so they have stood the test of time and aged quite nicely.

I also have a small, sturdy shed in the back of the garden, which originally held tools and other garden equipment. Since it looks like a miniature house, I turned it into a little bar. I installed lights, a counter, a small sink, a refrigerator, and a cabinet for storing stemware. Pretty bar-height chairs offer a comfortable place to chat while sipping a drink and enjoying the garden view. How nice to have a secret place nestled in the garden.

ARMILLARY SPHERE

This is a skeleton model of the celestial sphere, generally with the earth in the center. An outer ring shows the equator, poles, tropics, zodiacs, etc. Inner rings depict the sun, moon, and stars.

Garden Artifacts

Garden ornaments, such as statues, urns, fountains, sundials, massive olive jars, obelisks, and even birdhouses and dovecotes, are important components of a romantic garden—or garden room for that matter. I even use garden ornaments like these throughout my house, thereby bringing the outdoors in. Since ancient Greek and Roman times, and especially in Renaissance Italy, garden ornaments have played a crucial role in bringing structure and form to the landscape. That long history is one reason that garden statues are hot commodities on the auction market today—so you will most likely be competing against other eager gardeners when you make a bid.

Reproductions are a viable alternative to the genuine article, but do consider how special it is to add a piece of garden history to your own Eden. When shopping for old garden fixtures, look for unusual items that you think will hold their value (a little marketplace research goes a long way), because you will likely have to pay a substantial amount, given the popularity of garden decorations. And do not be put off by patina, signs of age, and even moss and dirt. These are all desirable features; after all, the item would have been sitting outside for some time and, in the process, aged and weathered naturally.

Any item you buy should be in good overall condition—although you can find bargains if you are willing to live with some chips and cracks (such defects can add to the charm of an item). Pieces having had major repair work, excessive restoration, or overly enthusiastic cleaning should be viewed with skepticism, too, since the value goes down when something has passed through too many meddling hands.

※ OPPOSITE: *The walkway is a grand path to my garage. The fixtures were bought new at a home center, but they've weathered beautifully and look rather antique, don't they?*

※ ABOVE: *A pretty maiden guards the cars and the roses.*

WENDY HOUSE

A small playhouse for children, often replicating the main house on the property. The name derives from a small house built for the character Wendy in the play Peter Pan, by J. M. Barrie.

✳ OPPOSITE AND ABOVE: *What was once a tool shed (and a pretty fancy one at that) is now a bar, perfect for entertaining alfresco. I had a counter, shelving, stools, and a small refrigerator and sink installed to make it fully functional. Guests are always immediately drawn there, whether or not I am serving drinks.*

Part Three

ROMANTIC
PROJECTS

Free time is at such a premium today. It seems almost foolish to expect any-one to take time to handmake decorative accessories that might seem easily bought in antique malls, home-furnishing centers, and linen superstores. Yet certain unique items are not so effortlessly locat-ed. Furthermore, the process of making something pretty for your home can be a personally rewarding one if you are so inclined. The resulting refurbished side table or handcrafted pillow not only adds a touch of romance to the room, but it also feeds your soul. It is well worth the investment of time and patience required.

Most important of all, when you create or trans-form an object, what you end up with is an item so unique, so personal, and so utterly distinc-tive that it becomes almost instantly a romantic heirloom. Imagine the delight your children, grandchildren, or favorite niece of nephew will surely experience when they inherit something pretty made with the love of your heart and the labor of your own two hands. That idea strikes a lovely cord—it's irresistible. So why not give one or two or more of the projects in the section a try? They may inspire you to learn a new skill, like sewing, or rediscover a talent you might have put to the side.

My collaborator on this project, Karen Kelly, has developed and written a series of projects inspired by many of the quintessentially roman-tic items in my home, and neither superior craft-ing nor home-improvement skills are required to complete them successfully. They are not exact copies of the items in my home; rather they cap-ture the spirit of my favorite items. Because the projects are not rigid replicas, they give you many opportunities to introduce your own decorating and color ideas to the mix. Each item can be cus-tomized to suit your décor.

Completing one or all of the projects will bring a very special, personal touch to your home, of course. Involving yourself in a creative project also frees your mind and elevates the soul. And what a relaxing and rewarding way to spend a quiet evening or a Saturday afternoon. While you work, think of all the lovely women and talented craftsmen of the past who enjoyed handcraft-ing beautiful things for their homes and loved ones—how romantic!

Chapter Eight

BEAUTIFUL BACKGROUND PROJECTS

While many wall and floor treatments, such as installing French doors or inlaying a marble floor, require the help of a professional, some projects are basic "do-it-yourselfers." If you are inclined and have some time to devote to painting or installing moldings, you can achieve beautiful, if not professional-grade, results and save quite a bit of money. It's a nice feeling to think that you had a true hand in decorating your home. Here are some quintessentially romantic decorating projects that create a soft background for your furnishings. All of the materials for these projects can be found at home-improvement and craft stores.

ADD DECORATIVE FRAME MOLDING TO WALLS FOR A PANEL EFFECT

Faux panels made with decorative trim molding (rounded and carved or fluted on the face side and flat on the back) break up expanses of wall space and add so much visual interest, drama, and architecture to a room. Keep scale in mind.

Wider wall moldings (3 to 5 inches) can be used in substantial rooms (16 by 20 feet and larger), while narrower styles (1 to 2 inches) might be better suited for smaller rooms. If you paint the moldings in the same color as the wall, elaborate carvings do not detract. If you like moldings carved to look like rope or vines, use them. Style is personal.

✳ BELOW: *Making sure that the 45-degree miter cuts are done precisely is the most important part of a professional result.*

MIRROR, MIRROR ON THE WALL

To add sparkle to a small room, such as a dining room, consider having mirrored glass cut to fit inside the molding. Use construction adhesive made especially for mirrors to securely attach the mirror to the wall. Or create a trumeau effect above a fireplace by attaching self-adhesive 12- by 12-inch beveled squares of glass above the mantel and then trimming the perimeter with a pretty molding. The beveling gives the wall a quilted effect.

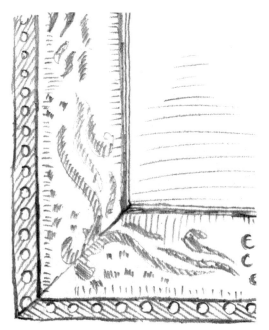

Trim molding in any style
or width you like

Decorative wood medallions
(optional)

Primer

Paint

Fine-grit sandpaper

Painter's tape

Graph paper (optional)

Tack cloth*

Construction adhesive
(optional)

Pencil

Miter box and saw

Level

Measuring tape

Hammer

Finishing nails

Nail set**

Tack cloth is a piece of cheesecloth soaked in a sticky substance that helps pick up fine dust from wood after it has been sanded. It's widely available and costs less than a dollar for one sheet.

**A nail set is a metal shaft with a narrow blunt point used to set nail heads below the surface of wood without denting the wood, by placing the blunt end on the nail head and hitting the other end with a hammer. You can find one in any hardware store for a few dollars.*

Directions

1. Decide where you want to place the molding, and measure the area. I have tall, almost floor-to-ceiling-length trim panels in many of my rooms, but you may want to create smaller panels on the lower third of your wall. It's completely up to you.

2. To make sure you have an even number of panels along the wall, measure the length of the wall and then divide it into four or five sections (for four or five panels). Space each framed area evenly within the sections. How large and how far apart the areas are spaced depend entirely on your personal preference and the length and height of your walls. For example, if you have an expanse of wall 15 feet long with a ceiling height of 10 to 12 feet, you might have four panels 3 feet wide and 6 feet tall spaced every 11 inches, if the molding is 1-inch wide. I recommend measuring first, then drawing in lines where the molding will be placed with a light pencil mark. Other ways to map out your plan would be to use a piece of graph paper (one square equals 1 foot) or place painter's tape on the wall to approximate panels until you find a design you like, then mark the edges of the tape as an installation guide.

3. Use a miter box and saw to cut the ends of each piece of molding at a 45-degree angle to create mitered corners.

4. Attach each piece to the wall using a hammer and finishing nails. Use a level to ensure that your moldings are installed straight. Before hammering the nail in completely, stop while the nail head is sticking out about $\frac{1}{8}$ inch and use a nail set to hammer it in flush with the trim. The nail set prevents the hammer from damaging the wood.

5. The center panel medallions in my music room are extremely ornate—you can get the same feeling with inexpensive wood or plaster medallions. Play around with your selected ornaments by attaching them with painter's tape. (They are light enough to stay on the wall while you decide what placement you like.) When you are satisfied with an arrangement, remove the painter's tape and attach the medallions to the wall. If you are applying wooden ornaments, use finishing nails to attach them. If you are applying plaster castings, use construction adhesive to attach them.

6. When you are done, sand the trim and wooden medallions lightly and clean them off with a tack cloth. Plaster ornaments don't need to be sanded. Then prime and paint the wall and trim as you like, or follow the glazing technique found later in this chapter.

PAINT AND GLAZE WALLS AND MOLDINGS

Antiquing glaze is a transparent tea-colored coating that mutes a painted finish and adds a hint of age without being obvious. The beauty of glazed walls reminds me of the great old estates and castles. The best results look natural, as if the walls have naturally aged to a pale, warm patina.

You never want to look at a glazed wall and say, "Oh look, a faux finish." In fact, the effect should be so subtle that you don't really notice the various layers of color. The variations of shades and tones should flow softly into one another. Buy the best quality paint you can afford. It's worth it, as your efforts will be rewarded with flawless coverage and a long-lasting paint job. Painting and glazing a wall with several layers of color is not a weekend project. One room may take you a week or more to complete. Don't rush; the walls won't look right if you do. Do one layer at a time, and keep building on it until you are satisfied with the results. The trick is using three shades of the same pale tone, one lighter than the next, on top of the base coat. If your ceiling is white, consider painting it in the base-coat color to blend with the overall effect.

COLOR BY DESIGN

If you can't find a color that's pale enough, you can lighten a close second by mixing it with 25 to 50 percent cream or white. (Start with the lesser amount and work your way up—you can add white, but you can't take it away.) Many large home centers now offer computer systems that can create an exact match to a swatch of fabric or a photograph of a favorite color. For example, you can use the photographs in this book to match colors.

✳ BELOW: *An old but clean cotton T-shirt is the perfect tool for applying the background paint in this project.*

Latex primer

Latex satin paint in linen or antique white for the base coat*

Latex satin paint in pale blue, pink, gray, or green (your preference) for the topcoat

Latex satin paint in one shade lighter than the pale blue, pink, gray, or green (your preference) above for the topcoat

Latex satin paint in one shade lighter than the topcoat above

Latex antiquing glaze

Bucket of clean water

One gallon of good-quality paint will cover an average-size 11 by 14 room.

TOOLS

Painter's tape

Fine-grit sandpaper

Canvas drop cloth

Paint tray and liner

9-inch roller suitable for flat surfaces and latex paint

2-inch paintbrush suitable for latex paint

Plastic paint buckets

Several soft, clean cotton T-shirts cut into squares

Directions

1. Wash and lightly sand all of the painted woodwork in the room, since you will be painting it in the same technique as the walls. If you prefer not to paint the trim, tape it off with painter's tape.

2. Prime the room, including the trim if you are planning on glazing it.

3. After the primer has dried (wait 24 hours), give the room one coat of the linen or antique white base coat.

4. Once the base coat has dried (wait 24 hours), dilute the first or darkest of the three light colors with water, using three parts paint to one part water, in a plastic paint bucket. Mix well.

5. Dip one of your T-shirt squares into the mixture and rub it on 4- by 4-foot sections of wall in a circular motion, being careful to clean up any drips before they dry. Because the paint has been mixed with water, the color will be sheer and uneven, meaning the base coat will show through more in some parts of the wall than others. This is the look you want—the surface color and texture should be slightly varied, giving a soft, cloudy look. Continue working in sections until you have the entire room done, including the woodwork and doors. Work from top to bottom and left to right as you move across a wall. Don't stop until you have completed one wall. Latex paint dries quickly and can create overlap marks. Let the room dry completely (overnight).

6. Follow the same procedure as described in Steps 4 and 5 for the next two shades, allowing each shade to dry before proceeding with the next shade. Use a new, clean T-shirt applicator each time you use a new color. Step back and look at your work occasionally. Some areas should be deeper in tone than others. If the wall starts to look too uniform, rub more topcoat on in certain areas—but don't let the variations become too delineated. Keep it subtle. Rinse out the cloth when it is saturated with paint, squeeze it out, and resume.

7. Once the final layer is dry, apply the antiquing glaze in the same fashion, using circular rubbing motions. The glaze unifies the layers and gives them an aged appearance without dramatically changing the color.

HAND-PAINT A WALL

After painting and glazing your room (page 166), you may want to embellish the walls further by adding a hand-painted swag or flowering vine. You can use a stencil, of course, but tracing a pattern you like onto the wall and filling it in with fine art paintbrushes and acrylic paints achieves a hand-painted result.

Use a pale palette that coordinates with the glaze, so that the result looks as if the painting has faded over the years. A gentle sanding when you are done furthers the aged look and softens the lines. If you like, you can practice painting your image onto a piece of watercolor paper or a canvas first. If you make a mistake while painting on the wall, just paint over it with the wall colors, let it dry completely, and start again.

❋ BELOW: *Use low-tack painter's tape to attach stencils to walls. It is easily removed and will not mar the paint job. You can also use a spray stencil adhesive, which allows you to reposition the stencil several times before reapplying the spray.*

MATERIALS

An image from a book or fabric you like (or use the one here); simple images are best for beginners

Transfer or graphite paper

Assorted acrylic paints

Antiquing glaze

TOOLS

Pencil

Painter's tape

Fine art flat-bristle paint-brushes, from ⅛ to ¼ inch

Fine-grit sandpaper or a clean white "scrub pad"

Soft, clean cotton T-shirt cut into medium-size squares

1. Choose an image you like and enlarge or reduce it on a copier to fit the space you are working in. Choose something fairly simple if you are a beginner. A vine with flowers, a swag of foliage and fruit, or an urn filled with roses might be good choices. Animal and human figures might be more challenging.

2. Use painter's tape to fix the transfer or graphite paper and the image to the wall, and trace all the lines with a pencil. When you lift up the paper, the image should be transferred to the wall.

3. Begin to paint. Fill in all large areas first and then work on fine lines. Don't worry too much about perfection, because you are going to sand and glaze over the painting, which will obliterate any errors or stray lines and create an aged, antique, romantic look.

4. When you are done and the paint has completely dried, lightly sand the painting to soften the color (best to wait until the next day for this step). Use fine-grit sandpaper or a new, clean white scrubber (the kind used to wash pots and pans). Colored scrubbers will leave color residue behind. Don't rub too hard. You do not want to completely remove the paint or risk damaging the wall.

5. Once you are satisfied with the look, use the squares of old T-shirt to lightly rub some of the antiquing glaze on top of the area of wall you painted, feathering the glaze out past the edges of the image to unify with the glazing that's already on the wall.

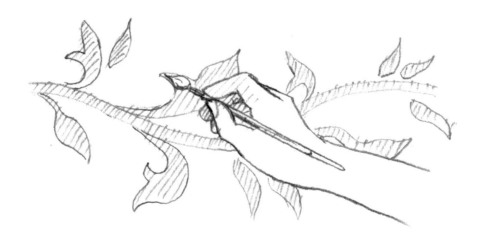

STENCIL A FLOOR

I love stenciled floors. The pretty vines and cherubs in my vanity room, which adjoins my bathroom, are done in a variety of soft pastels. It's my favorite floor in the house.

My floors were hand-painted, but you can achieve a similar result with a stencil and stencil paints. Look for solid oil-based stencil paints—they hold up better than regular acrylic craft paint under foot traffic—in a soft palette of two or three colors. Remember that vines don't have to be green; flowers don't have to be pink. A combination of dove gray and cream can be very pretty. Create a border around a room, or stencil a pretty flower or vine pattern randomly across the floor as I did, on any wooden floor in your home. I would not paint on top of tile or vinyl floors, as the paint will be more prone to wear on these nonporous surfaces.

✳ BELOW: *No need for expensive inlaid wood. Paint is an affordable way to give plain wooden floors a custom look.*

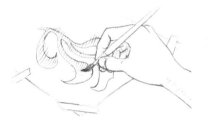

Directions

1. Decide where you want the images to go, and mark them off with a pencil. If you are scattering the stencil across the floor, make sure the patterns are evenly spaced. Use a tape measure to ensure even distances between the painted areas.

2. Use fine-grit sandpaper to gently sand the area of the floor where you plan to put your stencil. Sand in the same direction as the wood grain.

3. Clean the area with a tack cloth to remove dust, then clean the area with a lint-free cloth or old T-shirt dampened with a small amount of lacquer thinner.

4. Place the stencil on the floor and secure it with painter's tape.

5. Dip one of the stencil brushes into the paint, then gently tap it on a paper towel to remove the excess paint. You need only a very small amount of paint on the brush—a little goes a long way. Any excess paint will leak around the edges of the stencil and smudge the design.

6. Apply the paint using a gentle tapping motion. Build the color slowly, in light layers.

7. After you are done with one location, carefully remove the stencil and reposition it at the next spot with more painter's tape. Repeat the painting process until you are satisfied.

8. Allow all the painted areas to dry completely, following the manufacturer's instructions. Since it is oil paint, you may have to wait up to 48 or even 72 hours for it to dry completely.

9. Once the paint is completely dry, use fine-grit sandpaper to lightly sand the painting for a softer look. Clean up any dust with a tack cloth.

10. Protect the stencil with a coat of spray or brush-on polyurethane, especially in areas where there is a lot of foot traffic or where water might be spilled. Follow the sealer manufacturer's instructions for application and drying time.

ETCH OR FROST A WINDOW

A frosted panel of glass is lovely—light filters through it and creates an interesting dance of shadows on nearby surfaces. It's not difficult to transform ordinary windows into frosted or etched master-pieces, especially since glass-etching products are easier to use than ever and widely available at craft and home-improvement centers.

Until recently, the only way you could etch glass was with an acid-based etching cream that needed to be painted on and then rinsed off thoroughly in water (hard to do if you want to frost an already-installed window or door). Etching cream is difficult to use unless you are working on a flat surface. Spray-on glass-frosting products make it easy to achieve the look of frosted glass, and these products can be carefully removed by scraping them off with a razor blade when you tire of them or if you make a mistake. It's still a good idea to practice on a scrap piece of glass (perhaps from an old picture frame) to experiment with patterns and to perfect your technique. Try this simply romantic finish on bathroom windows, French doors, and glass-front kitchen cabinets.

MATERIALS

Glass-etching spray such as Window Etch

Stencil of your choice

Stencil spray adhesive

TOOLS

Glass cleaner

Lint-free cloth

Painter's tape

Directions

1. Use glass cleaner and a lint-free cloth to clean the surface you plan on etching.

2. Spray the back of the stencil generously with repositionable stencil adhesive, and apply the stencil to the glass, making sure that it is secure. Use painter's tape to cover any areas around the stencil or window that you do not want to etch.

3. Follow the manufacturer's instructions and apply the etching spray. Generally it is best done in light sweeping strokes.

4. When you are done, gently remove the stencil and allow the etching to cure for about one day before gently cleaning it with a damp cloth.

Chapter Nine

SOFT FURNISHINGS

Sewing is a precious and endangered skill at home. It seems everyone is so busy nowadays. Yet a pretty lace-edged pillow tossed on a club chair or a buttery velvet cloth draping luxuriously over a plain round table form and topped off with a circle of lace adds instant charm to a room and makes a thoughtful gift, too. Store-bought items can be costly, and finding exactly what you want could be a challenge. But if you make them yourself, you will save money and get exactly what you want. These decorating ventures require only basic sewing skills, a standard sewing machine (available at many discount department stores for about $75), and a modest investment of time. Even a beginner can achieve impressive results.

CREATE PRETTY PILLOWS

A plain, inexpensive linen, cotton, or velvet pillow of any shape is easily transformed into a one-of-a-kind heirloom with the addition of a scrap of vintage fabric, a lace doily, a square of tapestry, or even antique ribbon. This is such an easy project—do it at home while you watch your favorite romantic movie. And it is a wonderful way to show off special or sentimental pieces of fabric that would otherwise sit unused and unseen in a drawer. A pillow like this also makes a beautiful engagement, wedding, or anniversary gift.

Here are three ways to attach fabric to a ready-made pillow (depending on the kind of textile you are using).

1. Fuse on a Fabric Scrap

Fusible web, available at craft and sewing stores, makes attaching a scrap piece of fabric to a pillow very easy: All you need is an iron. Fusible web also gives additional support and body to fragile or lightweight fabrics. This is a perfect way to save and highlight a special piece of fabric taken from an old tablecloth, preserve the memory of a vintage dress that has outlived its usefulness, or use up small scraps of fabric.

MATERIALS

Pillow of any shape or size

Fabric scrap

Fusible web sized to fit your fabric scrap and appropriate for the fabric you are attaching to the pillow

Thread to match pillow and fabric

Pattern

TOOLS

Dressmaker's chalk

Sewing needle

Iron

Scissors

Straight pins

Pressing cloth

Directions

1. If possible, remove the pillow form from the case. This makes it a little easier to iron, but it's not necessary.

2. Press the scrap flat. Use one of the patterns shown on page 204, or make your own square, circle, heart, or rectangle to fit the scrap and the dimension of the pillow. For example, a triangle, square, circle, or heart would all look nice placed in the center of a round or square pillow. Use a copy machine to enlarge the pattern to suit your needs, and use the copy paper as a pattern to cut out the fabric.

3. Cut out the pattern adding $\frac{1}{2}$ inch all around for a hem. Pin the pattern to your fabric and cut it out. Use the pattern to cut out the fusible web without adding $\frac{1}{2}$ inch on as allowance.

4. Turn a $\frac{1}{2}$-inch hem and press it down with the iron. For folding a hem on rounded sides, as in the heart or circle shape, make small cuts $\frac{1}{4}$ inch into the hem allowance every $\frac{1}{8}$ inch on the curve.

5. Place the hemmed fabric on the pillow and make sure you are satisfied with the way it looks. To mark the position of the pattern, trace lightly around the fabric with the dressmaker's chalk, which is easily brushed away when you are done with the project.

6. Follow the manufacturer's directions for attaching the fusible web to the front of the pillow, and attach the appliqué to the front of the pillow with an iron where you marked with the chalk. Use a pressing cloth (a clean terry towel or another scrap of fabric will do) on top of the appliqué and pillow to prevent damage to the fabrics. Use the heat setting recommended by the web manufacturer's recommendations. It might be awkward to iron on top of a stuffed pillow, but it's not impossible.

7. As final "insurance," tack the appliqué down securely in a few spots with a couple of small stitches.

2. Appliqué a Lace Doily to a Pillow

Antique or new pieces of lace make a lovely embellishment to a ready-made pillow. Cotton crocheted lace is very sturdy, making it especially suited to this project. The small hand stitches make it easy to remove the lace for cleaning or if you want to replace the pillows with new ones but you still want to keep the lace.

MATERIALS

Pillow of any shape

Lace doily

Thread to match lace

TOOLS

Straight pins

Sewing needle

Directions

1. Arrange the lace on the pillow, and pin it in place with the pinheads facing out. Place pins every inch for security.

2. Use a needle and thread to tack the lace on, making small ($1/16$ inch) stitches all the way around the lace. If you have carefully matched the thread to the lace, the stitches will virtually disappear.

3. Appliqué Tapestry or Needlepoint

You can buy pillow-size pieces of tapestry or find vintage needlepoint from flea markets, and applying them to the front of a pillow is a great way to show them off. It's a very Old World look, perfect for a library, den, or drawing room. Choose a pillow with fringe trim or tassles for extra flair.

MATERIALS

Pillow of any shape

Tapestry or needlepoint to fit the pillow

Cotton sheeting (optional for needlepoint)

Thread to match tapestry

TOOLS

Straight pins

Sewing needle

Iron

Directions

1. If the tapestry or needlepoint needs to be hemmed, press the edges under about ¼ inch (or more) to fit on the front of the pillow. If you are using a piece of needlepoint and it is not backed, I recommend backing it with a piece of lightweight cotton sheeting. Cut it to fit the final size of the hemmed piece. Cut the edges of the needlepoint so ½ inch remains all around the needlework, and press it under so the pressed edges hold the backing temporarily in place.

2. Place the tapestry or needlework on the front of the pillow and pin it in place. Use a slip stitch (see below) to attach the piece to the front of the pillow.

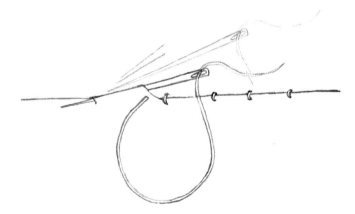

A SLIP STITCH IN TIME

To slip stitch, thread the needle with a double thread for strength. Hold the folded edge of the appliqué toward you, and work the needle from the right side to the left side. Bring the needle up through the folded side of the appliqué, and take a stitch into the pillow fabric directly opposite the point where the thread came out, catching just one or two threads of the fabric. Slip the needle through the fold a distance of about ¼ inch. Continue taking stitches about ¼ inch apart until the opening is closed. Tie a double knot in the thread, and trim as close to the knot as possible.

Renew a Pillow with a Pretty Cover

You can probably make two or three of these simple, lovely pillow covers in just a few hours. Use two sets of covers to shift the mood of a room as the seasons change (velvet for fall and winter, linen or ticking for spring and summer) or to coordinate with changes in bedding or dining room linens.

The secret to a professional result is to take your time and complete each step with care. Attention to the details, even simple ones, makes all the difference in the world. Take the time to measure accurately, sew straight lines, and press out seams.

I like the idea of covering an existing pillow with a piece of vintage brocade, embroidery, mattress ticking, or even lace. Pillow covers are a wonderful way to make use of old tablecloths, bed covers, and odd pieces of old toile or chintz. If you plan on using an old fabric, wash it by hand first with a mild detergent (Ivory Flakes are very good) and rinse it thoroughly.

If you use a length of lace or cutwork, and you don't want the existing pillow's fabric to show through, first back the piece with plain cotton or linen in a coordinating shade. In fact, it is a good idea to back any piece of vintage fabric you use (see below). It gives a delicate piece added strength and support.

A Firm Backing

To back fabric, simply line up the two lengths of fabric (following the measuring directions in Step 1 on page 179), and pin them together all the way around, making sure the right sides of both fabrics are facing up. Then sew the two pieces together as close to the edge as you can—about $1/8$ inch from the edge—all the way around. Press the piece. You now have a double-weight length of material.

MATERIALS

Vintage or new fabric, cleaned and pressed (and backed, if required)

Matching thread

Pillow form

TOOLS

Pinking shears or sharp fabric scissors

Sewing machine

Measuring tape

Iron

Directions

1. Measure the width and length of the pillow you will be covering. Cut the fabric 1 inch larger than the width and two times the pillow length plus 5 inches in length. A pair of pinking shears gives a fray-free edge, but if you don't have one, use a sharp fabric scissors.

2. Fold the narrow ends of the fabric over $\frac{1}{2}$ inch, two times for a clean edge, toward the wrong side of the fabric, and pin the hems. Sew them in place.

3. With the right side of the fabric facing up, fold in the right side and then the left side so they overlap in the middle. Pin the sides together and adjust as necessary using the pillow as a guide, so the finished length fits your pillow snugly but not so the fabric is taut.

4. Remove the pillow and sew the sides in place using a $\frac{1}{2}$-inch seam allowance. Trim the corners diagonally, leaving a $\frac{1}{8}$-inch seam on each corner (trimming reduces fabric bulk in the corners), and press the cover while it is still turned inside out. Iron the seams flat on a medium setting. Turn the cover right side out and press it again, using a pressing cloth, with the iron on a low setting so as not to damage delicate vintage or lace fabric. Slip the pillow into the cover.

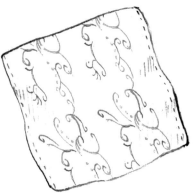

Trim a Throw Pillow with Lace or Fringe

If you feel more ambitious and want to make a stuffed pillow, it is just slightly more complex than the pillow slipcover. This one lets you add some lace or fringe trim. It's a good way to show off a ruffle of antique lace trim or crochet work or some luxurious fringe that might be too costly to use on a set of draperies.

You need only about 2 yards of the trim, so why not splurge on something really special? These pillows would look beautiful on a guest or master suite bed, chaise lounge, or even a settee or occasional chair in a living room.

✻ BELOW: *Go to town on lavish trims when making a pillow. Since you don't need a lot of material to complete the project, you can afford to splurge on fancy braiding, beading, silk tassels, and all manner of knotted and twisted fringes.*

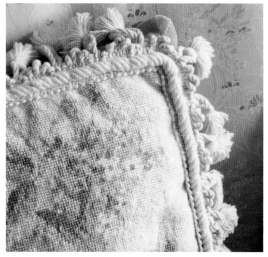

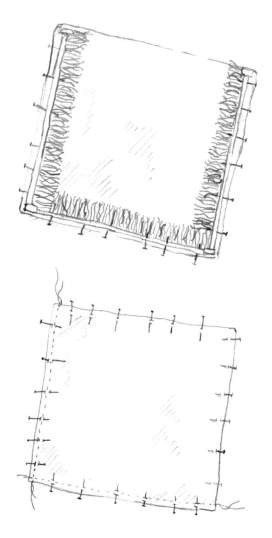

One 18-inch pillow form

$3/4$ yard of tapestry, ticking, chintz, or velvet to suit your décor*

$3/4$ yard of solid fabric to coordinate with fabric above (for example, if you are using tapestry, a solid or striped velvet might be nice; ticking might be pretty backed with a solid linen)*

Thread to coordinate with fabric

$2\,1/8$ yards of lace, crochet, or bullion fringe trim

* *The fabric should be at least 36 inches wide. You will have fabric scraps left from this project, which you can use to cover small cardboard boxes or plain journals.*

TOOLS

Scissors

Clear tape

Straight pins

Zipper foot for sewing machine**

Iron

Pressing cloth

** *The zipper foot is optional. Most sewing machines come with this standard attachment. Using it makes sewing easier, but you can still complete this project without one.*

Directions

1. Cut each fabric into 19- by 19-inch squares, which allows for an ample 1-inch seam allowance.

2. If you are using bullion fringe, tape each cut end to keep it from unraveling while you work. Pin the cording around the perimeter of the pillow front, touching the taped cord ends together. Place pins every 3 inches.

3. Cut away excess trim, leaving $1/8$ inch to turn under the lace or trim on each side, and pin the hem in place.

4. Sew the lace or trim to the pillow front with the zipper foot. Use the edge of the trim as a guide.

5. Place the back of the pillow on a flat surface, right side up. Position the pillow front on top of the pillow back, right sides together. Pin into place.

6. Use the trim seam on the pillow front as a guide to stitch the front and back of the pillow together. Leave a 6-inch opening in the middle of the bottom of the pillow for turning and stuffing the pillow. To make sharp corners, sew to the end of each side, remove fabric, and start the other side from the end, crossing the line you just stitched at a right angle.

7. Cut excess triangles of fabric off the four corners, leaving about a $1/8$-inch seam. Press the pillow before you turn it, pressing out the seams. Use the appropriate heat setting on the iron to match whatever fabric you are using. Use a pressing cloth with velvet, tapestry, or delicate fabrics.

8. Turn the pillow covering right side out and press it one more time using a pressing cloth as in Step 7.

9. Fold the pillow form in half, and gently work it through the opening. Smooth it out to fit in all corners.

10. Fold the raw edges under to match the existing seam, adjusting the trim so it's even with the sewn edges. Hand-stitch the pillow cover closed using a slip-stitch technique (see "A Slip Stitch in Time," on page 179).

COVER A ROUND TABLE WITH FULL-LENGTH FABRIC

A full-length tablecloth turns a basic 36-inch-round side table into an opulent setting for intimate formal dining or a glamorous table in a bedroom or living room on which to rest a glass of wine or a good book. In an entryway, a fabric-covered table is an elegant surface for a display of family photos, flower arrangements, or candles and other accessories.

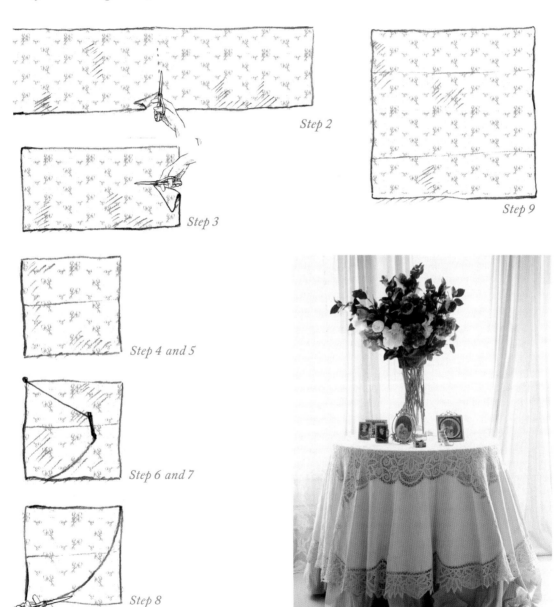

Step 2

Step 3

Step 9

Step 4 and 5

Step 6 and 7

Step 8

6 yards of decorator-quality 54-inch fabric in heavyweight velvet, silk, taffeta, or wool*

Fringe (optional)

Thread to match cloth

These 6 yards of fabric are enough to cover a 36-inch-diameter table that is 30 inches high. To determine the exact amount for your table, calculate as per Step 1 before buying fabric. If this is the first time you have embarked on a project like this and you are hesitant to cut up an expensive piece of fabric, make a practice version with a less expensive piece of cotton muslin, or use an inexpensive cotton round-table topper as a pattern (folding the round in quarters and placing it on your folded fabric).

TOOLS

Tape measure

Pinking shears

Sewing machine

Dressmaker's pencil

Safety pin

Cotton string

Pressing cloth

Straight pins

Sewing needle

Iron

Scissors or rotary cutter

Cutting pad (if you use a rotary cutter)

Directions

1. Determine how much fabric you need by first adding together the table's diameter and two times its height.

2. Use pinking shears to cut the fabric in half in the middle across the width, not the length, of the fabric.

3. Take one of the halves and use the pinking shears to cut it in half lengthwise.

4. Sew each of those half-width lengths to each side of the full-width piece to create a large square that is about 102 inches on each side. Use a standard $5/8$-inch seam when sewing.

5. Press the two seams flat, using a pressing cloth.

6. Fold the fabric in half and then in half again so you have a smaller square.

7. Make a compass by pinning one end of cotton string to the folded corner of the fabric and tying the other end to the dressmaker's pencil. Make sure the string is long enough to reach the outer edges of the fabric. Draw a quarter circle with the dressmaker's pencil along the outside edge of the square. The diameter of the arc should reach the edges of the fabric.

8. Use a scissors or rotary cutter and cutting pad to cut along the line of the arc.

9. Unfold the circle, and iron the cloth to remove the fold lines.

10. To hem, hand-sew a rolled hem. Check the width of the hem by placing the cloth over your table and pinning the hem up so that the fabric touches the floor or puddles on the floor (my round tablecloths puddle on the floor). Remove the cloths and then fold or "roll" the fabric over twice very narrowly and secure with a slip stitch (see "A Slip Stitch in Time," on page 179).

11. If you like, you can add fringe to the hem of the cloth. Attach it to the bottom right side of the cloth, and pin it securely in place with straight pins every 5 inches. With a straight stitch on a sewing machine, attach the fringe to the cloth (now that the cloth is hemmed by hand, it will be easy to control the fabric as you run it through the machine to attach the fringe).

12. Put the cloth on your table, and top it off with a round lace tablecloth or a square of crisp linen trimmed with lace.

Make a Floor-to-Ceiling Lace Swag for Your Bathroom or Bedroom

Beautiful and bountiful, a swag draping above the bathroom shower is a simple way to make a plain glass door very romantic. Wouldn't it be nice to start or end your day in a welcoming room like this? A swag is a snap to make.

Give New Lace an Antique Look

The crisp look of white or beige lace can be softened and antiqued with tea-dyeing. The Victorians used this method of staining lace and fabric. Put 3 black tea bags in 1½ cups of boiling water in a 2-cup bowl, and allow the bags to steep for 10 minutes. Remove them and carefully dip 2 to 3 yards of ½-inch-wide lace trim into the tea, using a spoon to gently submerge the lace. The lace should sit for about 15 to 30 minutes, depending on how dark you want the stain. Rinse thoroughly with cold water and allow the lace to dry on a clean, white, absorbent, terry-cloth towel or on the no-heat "air fluff" setting in the dryer.

If you want to tea-dye larger quantities of lace trim or dye lace yard goods (36- or 42-inch-wide lace bought by the yard, like any fabric), the procedure is the same but on a larger scale. Fill your sink or even the bathtub about halfway with the hottest tap water possible, and add 15 to 20 tea bags. Let them steep for 20 minutes, then add the fabric. Let it sit for up to an hour, then rinse with cold water and dry in your dryer, on the no-heat "air fluff" setting.

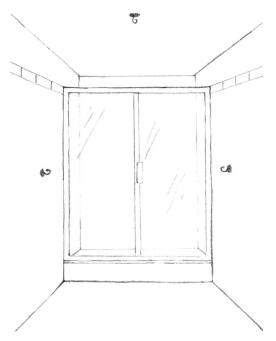

MATERIALS

Lace equal to double the height of your room, plus 4 yards

Two hanging plant hooks (approximately 2 inches)

One drapery or towel ring in the finish of your choice

White, cream, or ecru thread to match lace

2 yards of $\frac{1}{2}$-inch-wide satin ribbon to match the lace, cut into two 1-yard pieces

TOOLS

Sewing machine

Pinking shears

Iron

Directions

1. Following the manufacturer's directions, install the hooks on the facing walls (place the hooks about halfway up from the floor). Place the ring in the middle of the ceiling to form a triangle with the two hooks in the wall.

2. If you cannot buy a single length of fabric long enough for your needs (you may not find a full bolt of fabric and have to buy identical fabric off two bolts), sew two equal lengths together with a $\frac{1}{2}$-inch seam to create a single length. The seam will be hidden at the top of the swag, where it will "sit" on the ring in the ceiling. Trim the seam with pinking shears so the fabric will not fray, and press the seam out.

3. Hem each end of the lace by folding it over $\frac{1}{2}$ inch twice and straight-sewing it on a sewing machine.

4. Work the lace through the ring so it is even. Use the ribbons to tie the fabric to the hooks, then adjust the fabric so it drapes gently from the ceiling to the hooks and puddles a bit on the floor.

Alternative: Use lots of $\frac{1}{4}$-inch pastel-colored ribbons in 2-yard lengths to tie the lace to the hooks on each side to create a streamer effect.

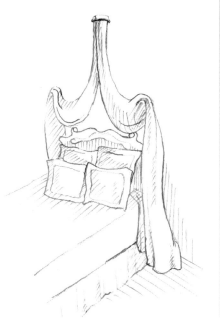

BED TIME

You can use the same pretty lace swag treatment over your bed. To calculate fabric quantity, measure the height of your wall and multiply it by 2, then add that figure to the width of your bed, plus 24 inches. (Measuring straight up the wall instead of at an angle toward the top center of the area above your bed gives you the excess fabric you need to create a soft swag.) Attach the top ring in the ceiling centered over your bed and about 12 inches in from the wall. Instead of using hooks on the sides of the bed, attach a coordinating drapery tieback (a metal or metal and porcelain or glass fixture that holds curtains in place) on both sides of your bed, about 12 inches away from each side. Look for tiebacks that come out straight from the wall and have decorative finials on the ends.

Chapter Ten

DECORATIVE ACCESSORIES
AND PAINTED FURNITURE

Soft furnishings are just part of the decorating story. A room layered with a range of accessories and decorative touches expresses your personality. Decorative accessories such as antique boxes and aged mirrors, gilt-covered occasional tables, and painted side chairs add the unexpected and a bit of sparkle and surprise to a romantic setting. It takes time to collect just the right pieces to layer in a room—and you may not ever find just the right piece. You can make many decorative items yourself. The ones here are surprisingly easy and fun to make.

PAINT A TREASURE BOX

A pretty way to store photos, ephemera, and mementos is in a decorative treasure box. I love boxes so much that I design them for my furniture line for American Drew. The bottom half of the one shown here is covered with gilt ormolu and is topped with an ornamental brass handle. It's finished in a stain I call bisque over maple wood.

While it would be difficult to make an exact replica of this box, it is easy to create a romantic treasure chest of your own with some basic finishing techniques. It's a pretty, neat, and discreet way to keep favorite memories nearby on a coffee table, bookshelf, nightstand, or desk. Use your imagination and make a box to suit your fancy— the instructions are very flexible.

A wooden box from a craft store in any size or shape you like (you can also use an old wooden box)*

Two-part brass or metal closures, or a hook and latch to match the handle (optional)

Hinges to replace those on the box in coordinating metal (optional)

Wood stain in any color you like

Stencils or images copied from a book or magazine

Transfer or graphite paper (if you use photocopied images)

Gold or other metal leaf and leafing size (optional)

Metallic craft paint in any color you like

Antiquing glaze

Colorless butcher's wax

Brass or metal handle in any decorative style you like (use a drawer pull or handle—look for antique or vintage handles at flea markets), sized to fit in the center top of the box

Look for a box with a lid that seems sturdy and is constructed with dovetail joints and nails instead of staples and glue—it will last longer. A hinged box is nice but not necessary.

Directions

1. The first thing you need to do is examine the box. If you are using an old or vintage box, it may very well have sturdy fixtures. However, if it's from a craft store, it is probably made of a soft pine and the hardware may not be terribly sturdy. If your box has a fitted top and no hinges or closures, move on to Step 2. If it does have metal fittings, examine them carefully. Sometimes the fittings are small and flimsy, even though the box itself is sturdy. This is why I think it is worth replacing the hinges and latch with sturdier versions found in the knob and pull section of home centers and hardware stores. If that is the case, remove the old hinges, and screw in the better-quality new ones (if you use the same size fittings, you do not have to drill new holes). Some boxes come with a small latch on the front side of the box. Again, if yours doesn't look like it will last very long (the brass is often thin and lightweight), take it off and attach a new one.

2. If you are using an unfinished box, lightly clean off the wood dust with a tack cloth. If you are using a vintage box and you like the condition and color of the finish, sand it lightly, clean it with a soft damp cloth, and dry it with a paper towel.

3. Stain the unfinished box inside and out with a stain of your choice, following manufacturer's instructions. I like light antique maple stain, but you can use any color stain that suits your décor. Let the stain dry completely, and if necessary, give it another coat to achieve the depth of color you want.

4. Now the fun begins. Add a decorative flourish to the bottom section of your box with metal leaf or metallic paint. Freehand a scroll pattern (like the one on my American Drew box), or use a pattern and transfer it onto your box with transfer or graphite paper and a pencil, then fill in the lines with paint. Let the paint dry, and then sand the box very lightly with fine-grit sandpaper, cleaning up any dust with a tack cloth.

5. When using metal leaf, follow the manufacturer's instructions. Generally, you apply a size first (size is a sticky liquid that adheres metal leaf to a surface) and let it cure until it becomes tacky (about 60 minutes), and then apply the sheets of leaf with a soft artist's brush. Metal leaf is very thin, so it can be challenging to use. Work inside with the windows closed (even a slight breeze can blow the sheet away). Each sheet will be lined with a piece of tissue paper.

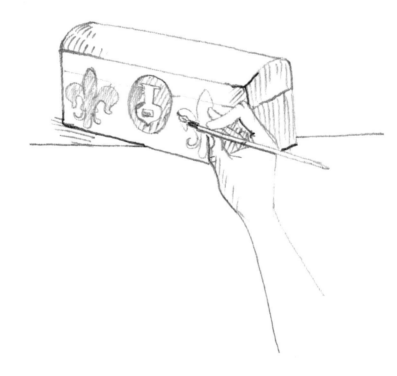

Fine-grit sandpaper

Tack cloth

Soft, damp cloth

Paper towels

Phillips-head screwdriver

Assorted flat-bristle artist's
paintbrushes

Rubber gloves

Old T-shirts for applying stain
and glaze and for waxing the
box

Power drill (optional)

Pencil

Use the paper and your brush to gently glide the metal sheet onto the box. Brush away any excess leaf with the brush, and burnish the leaf pattern with a soft, clean T-shirt by rubbing it gently in a circular motion.

6. Apply the antiquing glaze all over the box, following the manufacturer's instructions. Apply extra glaze to the corners and edges of the box for depth and to give it an aged look.

7. Let the box dry completely (2 to 3 hours), then apply butcher's wax to the outside, following the instructions on the side of the can. Waxing gives the box a warm, antique glow and water-resistant protective finish that simply cannot be achieved with polyurethane. It takes a little elbow grease, but since the box is not so big, it won't be difficult. (And you will be thrilled with the results.)

8. Now that the box is finished, top it off with a pretty handle. Look for one-of-a-kind knobs and pulls to make your box a truly unique object. Use a screwdriver to attach the handle, centering it on the top. If you are using a soft pine box, you should not have to predrill screw holes, but you also can't use a very heavy handle. Look for something light and delicate. But if you are using a hardwood box, a drill comes in handy for predrilling screw holes (use a drill bit that matches the width of your screw), and almost any metal handle can successfully be attached to hardwood.

MODIFY MIRRORS

Old mirrors have such an aura about them—it's as if friendly ghosts from another era were caught in the depth of their reflections. When you look into an old, spotted mirror, your image looks a bit cloudy, seen through the filter of times gone by. Old reflective glass may not be useful for putting on makeup or straightening your skirt, but it adds a soft gleam to a room and catches light in a very special way. Put a silver-leafed mirror or a collection of aged mirrors along or at the end of a narrow hallway, or group them in patterns on a wall for a dramatic effect.

CRAFT A SILVER-LEAFED MIRROR

Applying silver leaf to a piece of glass creates a very soft reflective surface. Such a mirror has limited practical application, but its decorative impact is stunning and authentically antique looking. You can even use this leafing technique to silver the glass panes of a French door—it offers privacy and elegance. Leafing supplies are easily found in craft and art-supply centers.

Directions

1. Remove the glass from the frame and clean the glass with glass cleaner and a lint-free cloth.

2. Follow the manufacturer's instructions to apply the leaf-sizing liquid to one side of the glass. The size has to dry to a tacky finish before you can apply the silver, and that generally takes from 30 to 60 minutes.

3. When the size is tacky, start applying the squares of silver leaf. Follow the maker's recommendations, which generally call for placing one sheet of leaf in the top left-hand corner of the glass, brushing it down with a soft artist's leafing brush or a clean blush brush, and continuing left to right until the glass is covered with the leaf.

4. Gently burnish the leaf with the brush, and gently rub it with the lint-free cloth. You will notice some spots where the leaf did not stick to the glass. Don't worry about this, because small open spots contribute to the vintage look of the finished product. If, for some reason, large areas are not covered, use the leaf scraps to fill them in.

5. Take the glass to a well-ventilated area. Holding the spray paint can about 12 inches from the glass, spray the leafed surface with one swift spray of gold paint. This will add subtle gold flecks to the mirror, which makes it look just a bit more authentic. Don't cover the leaf with the gold paint, and don't spray on more than one light coat.

6. Once the gold paint is dry (about 20 minutes), paint over the leaf with one coat of flat black paint. Allow it to dry, then fit it into your decorative frame. The ungilded reverse side of the glass should be facing out.

7. Place the glass back into the frame.

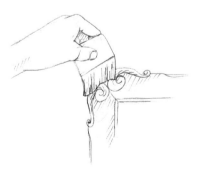

AGE AN EXISTING MIRROR

Collectors, antique dealers, and decorators love aged glass mirrors. It wasn't long ago that people sent old glass mirrors out to be resilvered so they looked new again, but now we all realize the value and beauty of an old piece of glass, flaws and all. You can age a new mirror to make it look like a flea market treasure with just a few simple tools.

MATERIALS

Lint-free cloth

Mirror

Frame to fit mirror
(mirror can already be framed)

Paint remover

TOOLS

Two small plastic dishes

Rubber gloves

2-inch paintbrush

Metal patina solution

Artist's flat-bristle paintbrush
or old toothbrush

Fine steel wool pad

Gold spray paint usable on
glass

Flat black acrylic craft paint

Plastic putty knife

Flat-head screwdriver

Clean, old towels

Directions

1. Remove the mirror from its frame by prying up the small metal triangular pieces (or sometimes small finishing nails) that hold it in place. Use a flat-head screwdriver and go slowly and be gentle. You don't want to break the mirror.

2. Place the mirror face down on a well-padded, covered work surface. Clean, old towels make a good resting spot for your mirror.

3. Most new mirrors have a flat gray protective coating over the silvering on the glass. You have to remove most of this to age the mirror. Put on rubber gloves and pour some of the paint remover into a plastic dish, and then use the 2-inch paintbrush to paint it onto the back of the mirror, covering most of the glass (you can leave a few spots alone).

4. Follow the recommended wait time indicated on the paint-remover can. Eventually the surface blisters and bubbles. At that point, you can take off the backing with a plastic putty knife. The paint remover will take off only the gray backing.

5. After you have removed the paint remover, if there is still some gray backing left, apply more paint remover and repeat the process. After the wait time, remove the second coating of paint remover with a fine steel wool pad. You don't have to remove every inch of the gray backing, but you should have removed most of it.

6. Clean the back of the mirror with soap and warm water, and dry it off with a lint-free cloth.

7. Pour some of the metal patina solution into a plastic dish and use an artist's paintbrush or an old toothbrush to gently flick it onto the back of the mirror. The little round spots replicate what really happens when a mirror ages over time by removing the silver in the areas it touches. If you use an old toothbrush, use your thumb to flick on the solution by running it across the bristles over the mirror. It does not take very long to work; follow the manufacturer's instructions for waiting time, and then wash off the solution under warm running water.

8. Dry the mirror with a lint-free cloth, and place it back face down on the padded, protected work surface. Spray the back of the mirror with one quick sweep of glass-friendly gold spray paint. After that has completely dried, spray-paint the back of the glass with flat black acrylic craft paint.

9. Once the black paint is completely dry, reframe the mirror and hang it up.

TRANSFORM OCCASIONAL FURNITURE

Small tables can be moved from room to room as the need arises. They make a nice perch for a cocktail or a vase of flowers. Side chairs are practical, too. Use them around a table for an intimate meal, or draw them into the living room for extra seating when friends visit. Incorporate these furnishings as a part of your romantic look; decorative treatments are accomplished with a few tools and a little patience.

Gently Distress a Painted Chair

The antique Swedish chairs in my garden room still retain much of their original paint. Painted chairs like these are coveted by collectors and can be hard to find these days. I found mine years ago when they were a little more available.

If your search for the perfect piece has ended in frustration, consider distressing an unfinished chair to achieve the feeling of a gently worn painted chair. It will not be an exact match to my garden room chairs, pictured below, but I hope you will use the photos to spark your imagination. Unfinished furniture is well made and very affordable. You can find almost any style of chair as well—from French provincial and Swedish style to American ladder-back. All of these styles would fit into a romantic room.

How Fair a Chair

Before waxing the chair, paint a pretty flower, vine, or fleur-de-lis on the front yoke of the chair in full-strength gray paint. When it's dry, sand it gently to soften the lines and then proceed with the wax finish. See template page 209.

❋ BELOW: *These chairs are antiques, but pine chairs from unfinished furniture shops are excellent candidates for this project. You'll have a vintage look in just a couple of hours.*

Unfinished pine chair

Water

Latex paint in soft dove gray*

Latex paint in a pale color
(My chairs are pale pistachio
green—but pale blue, blue gray,
creamy beige, or peach would
also work well.)

*One chair will use up about a
quart of paint. Use that as a
general guide when determin-
ing how much to buy. If you are
planning on painting four or six
chairs, buy a gallon of each color.
You will likely have leftover paint
that can be stored for future
projects, which is preferable to
running out of paint and having
to run to the store for more.*

TOOLS

Safety glasses, for sanding

Tack cloth

Several clean, old T-shirts cut
into applicator squares

Plastic paint buckets

Fine-grit sandpaper

Latex antiquing glaze

Butcher's wax

Directions

1. Gently sand the entire chair (even if it feels smooth) to remove any rough spots, then clean the dust off with a tack cloth. The sanding also brings the grain up to the surface, and this creates a nice texture underneath the paint and glaze.

2. In a plastic bucket, mix the gray paint with water in a 50-50 solution.

3. Use one of the T-shirt squares to rub the gray paint solution all over the chair. This will give the pine a weathered look, perfect as an undercoat.

4. When the gray paint has dried completely, transfer the quart of colored paint into another plastic paint bucket. Don't dilute it. Use another clean T-shirt square to thinly apply the colored paint to the chair.

5. When the colored paint is dry, sand some of it off with fine-grit sandpaper to give the chair a distressed, aged look. Sand in the areas where natural wear would occur, such as the back (where hands would pull the chair in and out under a table, for example), around the sides of the seat, and on the bottom of the legs. It's okay if some of the natural wood shows through; the antiquing glaze will tone it down.

6. When you are satisfied with the way the distressing looks as a result of your sanding job, rub on the antiquing glaze with another clean T-shirt square.

7. When the glaze has dried, wax the chair with a coat of butcher's wax, following the application recommendations on the can.

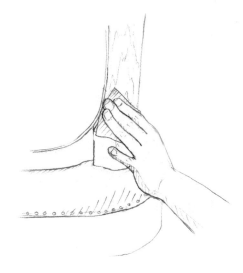

GILD A SIDE TABLE

A small occasional table can go from bland to beautiful with some carefully applied gold metal leaf and a marble top. I hope the padded one in my room inspires you (I use it as a piano stool, but with a hard top it would make a perfect table) to create your own unique piece.

If you are good at faux finishing, you can create a marblelike top with paint, but I think it is so much nicer to have a piece of real stone cut for the top of the table. Since you are using a small piece, a scrap from a stone supplier is all you need. It will be affordable, too. You might even find an old table that already has a marble top at an antique mall or flea market.

✳ BELOW: *Search craft stores and home centers for unusual wooden medallions. I love carved flowers, leaves, and small faces.*

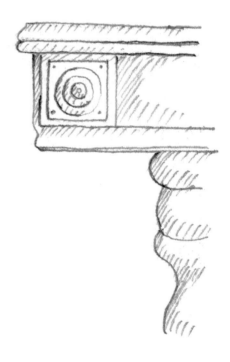

Directions

1. If you are using an unfinished table, sand it lightly and clean it with a tack cloth. If you are using a vintage table with paint, sand it. There is no need to strip it, but you need to sand it to remove loose paint and make sure it is smooth.

2. If you want to add decorative wood appliqués to a plain table, apply them with tack nails and some wood glue. They are easily applied to the sides of a straight table and can be applied to the flat leg fronts of round tables. Look for swags and medallions.

3. In a plastic bucket, mix four parts of red paint to one part of black paint to create a deep red.

4. Paint the table with the red paint mixture, watching for drips. Give it two coats, allowing it to dry between coats, and sanding it lightly after each coat has dried. Clean with a tack cloth. You are now ready to leaf.

5. Follow the manufacturer's directions for applying the size. You may have to do it in thirds, completing each third before moving on to applying size and then leafing the next section.

6. Apply the gold metal leaf with the brush, following the manufacturer's directions. Make sure to get into all the nooks of any carving or the appliqués. Use stray pieces of leaf to fill in holes.

7. When you are done, burnish the piece with a soft cloth. After that, you can seal the piece with acrylic sealer. This prevents the leaf from falling off and protects its finish (which is going to be soft, not shiny, with a matte-finish sealer).

Stencil Templates

Use these templates to create romantic projects at home, as noted in the captions. They can be enlarged or made smaller (depending on the size of the surface you are working on) using a standard copy machine. Or, get creative about how you use these motifs. For example, the fleur-de-lis silhouette below might be used to decorate a box, the back of a chair, a headboard, or even fabric. The decorative borders can adorn a wall, tabletop, or even the hem of a simple drapery panel. Use your imagination and have fun!

❊ USED IN CHAPTER 8: *enlarged templates on page 207*

❊ USED IN CHAPTER 9: *enlarged templates on page 208*   ❊ USED IN CHAPTER 10: *enlarged templates on page 209*

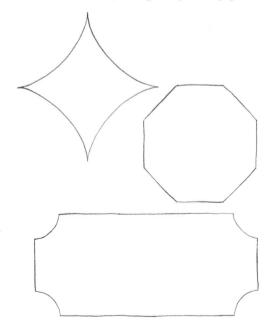

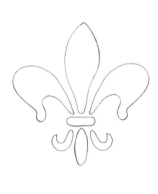

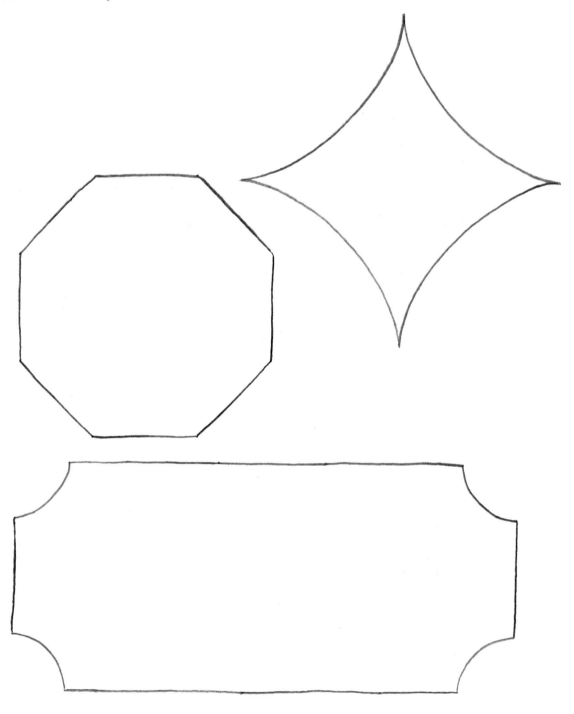

Resources

Jessica McClintock Furniture & Accessories

American Drew
4620 Grandover Parkway
P.O. Box 26777
Greensboro, NC 27417
www.americandrew.com

LEA Industries, Inc.
A La-Z-Boy Company
4620 Grandover Parkway
Greensboro, NC 27407
Telephone: 336-855-3393
www.leafurniture.com

LoLoi Rugs
4700 Alpha Road
Suite B
Dallas, TX 75244
Telephone: 972-503-5656
www.loloirugs.com

The Minka Group (JMC Lighting)
1151 W. Bradford Court
Corona, CA 92882
Telephone: 951-735-9220

Staircase Mural

Roxana Santos de Hayden
928 Springview Circle
San Ramon, CA 94583
Telephone: 925-551-3788

Bedroom and Atelier Painting

Impressions in Paint
1190 Koch Lane
San Jose, CA 95125
Telephone: 408-286-4460

Architects

Ted Eden and Diane Burn
Telephone: 415-956-3640 x12

Mantelpieces

Bill Sullivan, master carpenter

Construction

Gunnell Construction
Robert Gunnell
71 Shell Road
Mill Valley, CA 94941
Telephone: 415-389-1340

Flowers

Podesta Baldocchi
Stephanie Brodene, head designer
Mollie Pence, designer
410 Harriet Street
San Francisco, CA 94103
Telephone: 415-346-1300

Chandeliers

Livio, Giovanni & Zoppi Alessandro
San Marco 2070/a
30124 Venizia, Italy

Acknowledgments

I send heartfelt thanks to
my brother Jack Hedrich and to Kerry Glasser.

Many thanks also to Diane Burns and Ted Eaton
for helping me to express my vision of a beautiful home.

— Jessica McClintock

I would like to thank Cathy Repetti, Jennifer DeFilippi,
Margot Schupf, and Marianne Paul for their valuable input.
Many thanks to Jessica McClintock for giving me the opportunity
to enter into her amazing world and write about it.

Thank you to my mother and father
for giving me a sense of and appreciation for beauty.

— Karen Kelly

Index

Underscored page references indicate sidebars.

Boldface *references indicate photographs and illustrations.*

A

Accessories
  bathroom, 122, 128
  bedroom, 112, **112**, 113, 119, **120**
  living room, 59, 74–75, **74**, **75**, **76**, 77, **77**
  seasonal changes of, 52
Accessories projects, 188, **189**
  aging an existing mirror, 198–99, **198**, **199**
  crafting a silver-leafed mirror, 196–97, **196**
  modifying mirrors, 194, **194**, **195**
  painting a treasure box, 190–91, **190**, **192**, 193
Alençon lace, 111
Alyssum, 153
American service, as table setting, 95
Antique stores
  beds from, 106
  doors from, 29
  fireplace surrounds from, 40
  perfume bottles from, 128
  rugs from, 74
  upholstered furniture from, 57
  vintage commercial items from, 86
Appliances, kitchen, 86, **87**, **88–89**, 89
Appliquéing
  of lace doily to pillow, 178, **178**
  of tapestry or needlepoint to pillow, 179, **179**
Appliqués, on walls, 35
Arch, in garden room, 146
Architects, 26, 29, 36
Architectural details, 36, 37, 146
Architecture, as inspiration for home décor, 8
Area rugs. *See* Rugs
Armillary sphere, 155
Armoire
  for bathroom storage, **125**, 128
  for guest room, **117**, 119
  for hiding electronics, 113
  for kitchen storage, 84, **85**
Art, as inspiration for home décor, 6
Art Deco style, characteristics of, 13
Art Nouveau style, characteristics of, 13
Asian arch, in garden room, 146
Asymmetrical arrangements, 18
Atelier, 140–42
Aubusson rugs, 73, 73, 74, 106, **109**

Auctions
  beds from, 106
  rugs from, 74
  shopping at, 77

B

Background projects, 162, **162**, **163**
  decorative frame molding for panel effect, 164–65, **164**
  etching or frosting a window, 172–73, **172**, **173**
  hand-painting a wall, 168–69, **168**, **169**
  painting and glazing walls and moldings, 166–67, **166**
  stenciling a floor, 170–71, **170**
Backgrounds
  doors, 24, **24**, **25**, 26, **28**, 29–30
  fireplaces, **38**, 39–40, **41**, 42, **42**
  floors, 43, **43**, **44**, 45, **45**
  hardware, 31, **31**
  importance of, 22
  moldings, 32, **32**, **33**, 35, 36–37, **36**, **37**
  panels, 32, **33**, **34–35**, 36
  wall painting, **46**, 47–49, **47**, **48**, **49**
  windows, 24, 26, **26**, **27**, **29**, 30, **30**
Balance, in romantic decorating, 18
Baldachin, 108, **108**, **108–9**, 116, **116**, 119
Balloon-back chairs, **94**
Bar, in garden shed, 155, **159**
Baroque style, characteristics of, 12
Baskets, for storage, **126**, 127, 142
Bathrooms
  guest, 130–31
  making lace swag for, 186–87, **186**
  master, 122–29
Bathtubs, 122, **123**, 124
Battenberg lace, 122
Beams, kitchen, 37
Bed linens, 108
Bedrooms
  children's, 115
  guest, 116–21
  making lace swag for, 187, 187, **187**
  master, 106–13
Beds
  for children's rooms, 115
  daybeds, 115, 143, 143, **143**
  feather, 111

for guest rooms, 116, **116**, **118**, 119, **119**, 120, **120**
  for master bedroom, 106, **107**, 108, **108–9**, 111
  mattresses for, 111
Bench, bedroom, **121**
Bergère chairs, 59, 62, 66, 112
Boiserie, 36
Bonheur du jour, 141
Books, as inspiration for home décor, 2, 4, **9**
Boudoir, 106
Boudoir pillow, 114
Bouillotte lamp, 68, 69, **69**, 70, 106
Boxes, as accessories, 74, **74**, 75, **76**, 77
  painting, 190–91, **190**, **192**, 193
Brocade, 64
Budgeting considerations, 51
Burns, Diane, 80, 116, 141

C

Cabinets, kitchen, 84, 86
Candlelight, 70, 99
Candles, 99
Candytuft, 153
Canopies, bed, **49**, **108**, **108–9**, **110**, **116**, 119, 120
Cardinal climber, 152
Carpeting, wall-to-wall, 45. *See also* Rugs
Cast iron, 134
Ceilings
  painted, 83
  raising, 26
  visually lowering, 36
Chair rails, 32
Chairs
  antique
    inspecting, 94
    size and comfort of, 54, **54**
  arranging, in living room, 60, 62
  bathroom, **122**, 124, 128
  bedroom, 112, **112**, 119, 120
  bergère, 59, 62, 66, 112
  dining room, **91**, 93
    styles of, 94
  fauteuil, 94, 112
  garden room, 144
  for man's office, 142
  oversize, 56
  painted, distressing, 202–3, **202**, **203**
  side, uses for, 200
Chaise, 119, 143

Chandeliers
    atelier, 142
    bathroom, 127
    bedroom, 106
    dining room, 90, **91**, 93
    kitchen, **82**, 83, 84
    living room, 69, **71**
    staircase, **70**
Chantilly lace, <u>113</u>
Chest of drawers
    bedroom, **110**, 112
    mirrored, 72
Children's rooms, 115
China, 97, 99
Chintz, 64, 65
Clematis, <u>152</u>
Clocks, 74, **75**
Coffee table
    arranging, in living room, 60
    arranging accessories on, 77
Color
    of furniture wood, 56
    in monochromatic palette, **20**, 21
    paint, lightening, <u>166</u>
    of upholstery fabrics, 56, 59
Color schemes
    for children's rooms, 115
    fabric swatches and, **11**
    for garden plants, 151, 154
    for man's office, 142
    for walls, 47–48
Columns, 37
Comfort
    bedroom, <u>111</u>
    furniture, 54, **54**
Conservatory, <u>144</u>
Containers
    for flower arrangements, 100, 104
    for garden plants, **148–40**, 150, **151**
Continental service, as table setting, 95
Coppola, Francis Ford, 22, 62, 80, 137, 148, 150, 151
Cornices, 37
Couch, <u>143</u>
Covers, pillow, making, 180–81, **180, 181**
Cremone bolt, <u>31</u>
Crown moldings, 36
Curtains
    bathroom, 127
    changing, 65
Cutting room, 137, **137**
Cypress vine, <u>152</u>

D

Damask, 64
Daybed, 115, 143, **143**, <u>143</u>
Daydreamy corners, 143
Decanting wine, <u>139</u>, **139**
de Hayden, Roxana Santos, 134, 137

Design decisions, freedom in making, <u>5</u>
Design journal, purpose of, 11, **11**, 65
Desks
    living room, 62, **63**
    office, 140, **140, 141**, <u>141</u>
de Wolfe, Elsie, 32, 35, <u>77</u>
Dimmers, for adjusting lighting, 69, 90, 106
Dining rooms
    family meals in, 78
    furniture for, 90–94
    history of, 78
    modern-day use of, 80
    table settings for, 94–99
Dining sets, vintage, 93
Dishwasher, panel covering, 86
Doors
    as background, 24, **24, 25**, 26, **28**, 29–30
    closet, 141
    entryway, 132, **132**
    etched glass in, **30**, 127, **127**
    French, **24, 25**, 29–30
    frosted glass in, 29–30, **30**
    lace panels for, 83
    retrofitted, **25**, 29
    shower, **25**, 127, **127**
    wood-paneled, 29
Draperies
    fabric choices for, 65, 66
    seasonal changes of, 52
Dresser, bedroom, 115, **115**
Dress form, 141–42, **141**

E

Electronics, hiding, in armoire, 113
English ivy, <u>152</u>
English service, as table setting, 95
Entryway, 43, 45, 132–33
Etching technique, for window, 172–73, **172, 173**
European pillow, <u>114</u>

F

Fabrics
    attaching, to pillows, 176–79, **176, 178, 179**
    backing, <u>180</u>
    covering round table with, 184–85, **184**
    for draperies, 65, 66
    draping, on dress form, 141–42
    romantic, types of, 64–65, 66–67, **66, 67**
    texture of, 21, **21**
    for upholstered furniture, 56, 59, 65, **65**, 66
Fabric swatches, purpose of, **11**, 65
Fashion, as inspiration for home décor, 5–6, **6, 7**
Fauteuil chairs, <u>94</u>, 112
Feather beds, <u>111</u>

Ferns, <u>153</u>
Fireplaces, **38**, 39–40, **41**, 42, **42**
    accessories for, 42, **42**
    faux, 62
    furniture arrangement with, 60, 62
    trumeau effect above, 39, 119, <u>164</u>
Fireplace surrounds, **38**, 39, **39**, 40, **41**
Floors, 43, **43**, **44**, 45, **45**
    bathroom, 122, **124**, 127
    bedroom, 106
    dining room, 90
    entryway, 43, 45, 132, **133**
    garden room, 45, 144
    kitchen, 83
    parquet, <u>45</u>, **45**
    stenciling, 170–71, **170**
Flowers
    arranging, 100, **100, 101, 102**, 103–4, **103, 104, 105**
    in bathroom, 124, 128
    in bedroom, 112, **112**, 119
    in garden, 150, 151, 154, **154–55**, 155
    in seasonal decorating, 52
Focal point, creating, 62, 64
Fragrances, home, 130
Friezes, 32
Fringe, trimming pillow with, 182–83, **182**
Frosting a window, technique for, 172–73, **172, 173**
Fruit stand, in garden room, 144
Furniture. *See also specific rooms and furnishings*
    antique, desired condition of, 52, <u>94</u>
    arrangements of, 60, **60, 61**, 62, **62, 63**, 64
    mirrored, 72
    new, desired construction of, 52
    occasional, painting, 188, 200, 202–5
    selection considerations for
        color, 56, 59
        comfort, 54
        construction, 52
        size, 54, 56
        upholstery, 52
    upholstered
        choosing, <u>57</u>
        fabric choices for, 52, 56, 59, 60, 65, **65**, 66
Fusible web, 177

G

Garden, 148–51, 154–59
    artifacts for, 157, **157**
    vines and trailing plants for, <u>152–53</u>
Garden room, 45, 144, 145, **145**, 146, **146, 147**
Glassware, **98**, 99

Glazing
 of architectural details, 37
 of mismatched furniture, 93
 of stove hood, 89
 wallpaper with, 48
 of walls, 24–25, 48, 49, 83, **83**, 90, 106
Gothic Revival style, characteristics of, 13
Guest bathrooms, 130–31
Guest bedrooms, 116–21

H

Hand-painting
 of floors, 37, 43, **43**, 45
 of moldings, 37
 of walls, 106, 168–69, **168**, **169**
Hardware, 31, **31**
Hepplewhite chair, 94
Home office, 140–42

I

Inspiration, romantic, sources of, 1–2, 4–10
Interior designers, 5, 11, 26, 29, 36
Ironwork, 134, 134, **134**

J

Japanese honeysuckle, 152
Journal, design, purpose of, 11, **11**, 65

K

Kelly, Karen, 161
King pillows, 114
Kitchens
 appliances in, 86, **87**, **88–89**, 89
 beams and cornices in, 37
 designing, 80, 83–84
 history of, 78
 modern-day use of, 80
 storage options in, 84, **85**, 86, **86**
Kitchen staff, 80

L

Lace, 66–67
 Alençon, 111
 for bathroom, **127**
 Battenberg, 122
 for bedroom, 108
 Chantilly, 113
 tea-dyeing, for antique look, 186
 trimming pillow with, 182–83, **182**
 Venice, 119
Lace doily, appliquéing, to pillow, 178, **178**
Lace swag
 for bedroom, 187, 187, **187**
 for shower, **131**, 186–87, **186**

Lace table coverings, 97–98, 99
Lamps
 bouillotte, **68**, 69, **69**, 70, 106
 for man's office, 142
 table, 70
Light, natural
 increasing, 22, 24, 29–30, **30**
 reflected from mirrors, 72
Lightbulbs, for adjusting lighting, 69
Lighting, artificial. *See also specific fixtures*
 in atelier, 142
 in bathroom, 127, 128
 in bedroom, 106
 dimmers for controlling, 69, 90, 106
 in dining room, 90, 93
 in kitchen, 83–84
 in living room, **68**, 69–70, **69**, **70**, **71**
Linens
 bed, 108
 table, 97–99
Lines, straight vs. curvy, 25
Literature, as inspiration for home décor, 2, 4, **9**
Little Prince, The, 2, 4
Living rooms
 accessories for, 59, 74–75, **74**, **75**, **76**, 77, **77**
 fabric choices for, 64–67, **65**, **66**, **67**
 furniture arrangements in, 60, **60**, **61**, 62, **62**, **63**, 64
 lighting for, **68**, 69–70, **69**, **70**, **71**
 mirrors in, 72
 in modern homes, **58**
 rugs in, 73–74, **73**
Louis Seize style, characteristics of, 12, 13
Loveseat, 56
Luxury, in romantic decorating, 14, **14**, 17

M

Man's office, 142
Mantels
 over bathroom sink, **126**, 127
 fireplace, 42, **42**
Marble floors, **44**, 45, **45**, 122, 144
Marquetry, 90, **90**
Mattress, 111
McClintock, Jessica, **3**, **7**, **9**, **10**, **140**
 as fashion designer, 1, 5–6, **7**
 home of, 8, 22
  atelier in, 140–42
  bathroom in, 122–29
  cutting room in, 137
  daydreamy corners in, 143
  dining room in, 90–93
  doors in, 24, **24**, **25**, **28**
  drawing room in, 52, 60–62, **63**, 65–66

 entryway in, 132–33
 exterior of, **8**, 22, **23**
 fabric choices for, 65–66
 fireplaces in, 39–40
 floors in, 43, 45
 garden of, 148–51, 154–59
 garden room in, 144–47
 guest bathroom in, 130–31
 guest bedrooms in, 116–21
 interior design of, 12, 22, 24–25
 kitchen in, 37, 45, 80–89, 84, **85**, 86, **86**
 lighting in, **68**, 69–70, **70**, **71**
 living room arrangements in, 60
 master bedroom in, 106–13
 moldings in, 32, **32**, **33**, 37
 music room in, **22**, 52, 56, 59, 60, **62**, 66, **71**, 72, 73, 74
 staircase in, 45, 134–37
 wall color in, 47, 48–49
 windows in, **26**, **27**, 30
 wine cellar in, 138
 sources of inspiration for, 2, 4–10
McGill, Amy, 127
Meals, serving, 78
Medallions, 36, 37
 on floor, 43, 45
 on side tables, **204**
 on stove hood, 89
 on walls, 32, 165
Memoirs of a Geisha, as inspiration for home décor, 4–5
Mirrors
 aging, 198–99, **198**, **199**
 bathroom, **126**, 127–28, 130
 bedroom, **110**, 112
 over fireplace, **38**, 39, **40**, **41**
 as focal point, 62, 64
 in garden, 154
 inside molding, 164
 old, for decorative effect, 194, **194**, **195**
 reflecting light, 72
 silver-leafing, 196–97, **196**, **197**
Moldings
 as background, 32, **32**, **33**, **35**, 36–37, **36**, **37**
 choosing size of, 37
 highlighting, 25
 painting, 37, 47, 49, 166–67, **166**
 for panel effect, 164–65, **164**
 ready-made vs. custom-made, 36
 rinceau in, 35
Monochromatic palette, in romantic decorating, **20**, 21
Moonflower, 152
Morning glory, 152
Movies, as inspiration for home décor, 4–5
Mozart, 4, **5**

Murals
    on staircase wall, **48**, 49, **49**, 134,
      135, 137
    wallpaper, 137
Music, as inspiration for home
    décor, 4

N

Naming rooms, 52
Nature, as inspiration for home
    décor, 8, **10**
Neck roll, 114
Needlepoint, appliquéing, to pillow,
    179, **179**
Nesting tables, mirrored, 72, **72**
New World, The, as inspiration for
    home décor, 5

O

Openness, in romantic decorating,
    22, 24, 26
Ormolu, 74, 75, 75

P

Painters, finding, 49, 137
Painting
    choosing colors for, 47–49, 122
    floors, 43, **43**, 45
      with stenciling, 170–71, **170**
    glazing (*see* Glazing)
    hand-painting, 106, 168–69, **168**,
      169
    lightening color of, 166
    of moldings, 37, 47, 49, 166–67
    with strie technique, 119
    of walls, 24–25, 37
Painting projects, 200, **200**, **201**
    distressing a painted chair,
      202–3, **202**, **203**
    gilding a side table, 204–5, **204**
    painting a treasure box, 190–91,
      190, **192**, 193
    stencil templates for, 206,
      206–9
Panels
    appliance, 86
    frame molding for creating,
      164–65, **164**
    wall, 32, **33**, **34–35**, 36, 72, 77
Parquet floor, 45, **45**
Perfume bottles, 128, **129**, 130, **131**
Pets, as inspiration for home décor,
    8, 10, **10**
Photographs, displaying, **9**, 62, 74,
    112, 113
Piano, 4, 60, **62**
Picture frames, 77, 113
Picture railing, 36, **36**
Pillows
    attaching fabric to, 176–79, **176**,
      178, **179**

bed
    arranging, **113**
    types of, 114
    fabric for, **67**
    making covers for, 180–81, **180**,
      181
    seasonal changes of, 52
    trimming, with lace or fringe,
      182–83, **182**
Plants. *See also* Flowers
    in garden room, 144, 146
    trailing, vines and, 152–53
Plinths, 60, 62
Polk, Willis, 12
Pool, reflecting, 148, **148–49**, 150,
    151
Porcelain, 98
Powder room, 130
Projects, romantic
    background, 162, **162**, **163**
      decorative frame molding
        for panel effect, 164–65,
        164
      etching or frosting a window,
        172–73, **172**, **173**
      hand-painting a wall, 168–69,
        168, **169**
      painting and glazing walls
        and moldings, 166–67, **166**
      stenciling a floor, 170–71,
        170
    decorative accessories, 188, **189**,
      194, **194**, **195**
      aging an existing mirror,
        198–99, **198**, **199**
      crafting a silver-leafed
        mirror, 196–97, **196**, **197**
      painting a treasure box,
        190–91, **190**, **192**, 193
    inspiration for, 161
    painted furniture, 188, **188**, 200,
      200, **201**
      distressing a painted chair,
        202–3, **202**, **203**
      gilding a side table, 204–5,
        204
    rewards from, 161
    soft furnishings, 174, **174**, **175**
      attaching fabrics to pillows,
        176–79, **176**, **178**, **179**
      covering round table with
        full-length fabric, 184–85,
        184
      making lace swag for
        bathroom or bedroom,
        186–87, **186**, **187**
      making pillow covers, 180–81,
        180, **181**
      trimming pillow with lace or
        fringe, 182–83, **182**
Proportion
    in romantic decorating, 18, **19**,
      20, **20**
    room, furniture size and, 56

Q

Quality, in romantic decorating, **16**,
    17, **17**, 51
Queen pillow, 114

R

Railings, staircase, 134, **134**
Recamier, 52
Reflecting pool, 148, **148–49**, 150,
    151
Refrigerator, housing for, 86, **87**
Reproductions
    of fireplaces and surrounds, 40,
      42
    furniture, 54
    of garden ornaments, 157
Rinceau, 35
Rococo style, characteristics of, 12
Romantic decorating
    budget considerations in, 51
    characteristics of, 1, **2**
    decision making in, 51
    principles of, 14–21
    sources of inspiration for, 1–2,
      4–10
    styles of, 12–13
    taking time with, 51
Romanticism, impact of, 8
Rugs, 45, 73–74, **73**
    Aubusson, 73, 73, 74, 106, **109**
    Savonneries, 73
Russian pillow, 114
Russian service, as table setting, 95

S

Salvage yards
    architectural details from, 146
    doors from, 29
    fireplace surrounds from, 40
    streetlights from, 151
    vintage commercial items from,
      86
    vintage moldings from, 36
San Francisco, 8, 39, 143, 154
Savonneries, 73
Scale, of enlarged windows and
    doors, 26
Sconces
    bathroom, 128
    bedroom, 106
    dining room, 93
    garden room, 144, 146
    kitchen, 83, **83**
    living room, 69–70, **70**
Screen, for creating private room,
    143
Shed, garden, 155, **159–60**
Shield-back chairs, 94
Shower, guest room, 130, **130**
Shower swag, 130, **130**
    making, 186–87, **186**

Sideboard, 93, <u>93</u>, 144
Side tables
    arranging, in living room, 60
    gilding, 204–5, **204**
Silk, 64
Silver leaf, applying, to mirror,
    196–97, **196, 197**
Sink
    bathroom, **126**, 127, 130
    kitchen, 84, 86, **86**
Size, of furniture, 54, 56
Slip stitches, 179, <u>179</u>, **179**
Small rooms, enlarging look of, 26
Sofas
    arranging, in living room, 60, 62
    fabrics for, 65, **65**, 66
    oversize, 56
    reupholstering, 52
Soft furnishings projects, 174, **174,**
    175
    attaching fabrics to pillows,
        176–79, **176, 178, 179**
    covering round table with full-
        length fabric, 184–85, **184**
    making lace swag for bathroom
        or bedroom, 186–87, **186,**
        187
    making pillow covers, 180–81,
        180, 181
    trimming pillow with lace or
        fringe, 182–83, **182**
Sophistication, in romantic
    decorating, 14, **15**
Stain removal, for table linens, 98
Staircase, 134–37
Standard pillow, <u>114</u>
Statues
    bathroom, **124, 128, 129**
    garden, 157, **157**
    music room, 4, **5**
Stenciling, floor, 170–71, **170**
Stencils, 49
    templates, 206, **206–9**
Stonework floors, 45, 144
Storage
    baskets for, **126**, 127, 142
    bathroom, **125, 126**, 127, 128
    built-in, 141
    kitchen, 84, **85**, 86, **86**
Stove, 86, **88–89**, 89
Stove hood, 86, **88–89**, 89
Streetlights, in garden, 150–51, **150**
Strie, 119
Sweet pea, <u>152</u>
Sweet potato vine, <u>152</u>
Symmetry, 18, **18**, 60

Table lamps, 70
Table linens, 97–99

Table manners, <u>95</u>
Tables
    bathroom, 124
    bedroom, 112, **112**, 119, 120
    coffee
        arranging, in living room, 60,
            60, 62
        arranging accessories on, 77
    covering with full-length fabric,
        184–85, **184**
    dining room, 90, **90, 91**, 93
    garden room, 144
    mirrored nesting, 72, **72**
    side
        arranging, 60
        gilding, 204–5, **204**
    small, uses for, 200
    vanity, in bathroom, 128, **129**
Table settings, 94–99, **95, 96, 97,**
    98, 99
Taffeta, 64
Tapestry, 64
    appliquéing, to pillow, 179, **179**
Televisions, concealing, 113
Texture
    of fabrics, 66
    in romantic decorating, 21, **21**
Tile floors, 45, 83, **83**, 122
Toile de Jouy, 64–65
Toilet, 130, **131**
Trailing plants, <u>153</u>
Transfer ware, <u>97</u>
Travel pillow, <u>114</u>
Treasure boxes. See Boxes
Trellis, garden, 155
Trims, pillow, 182–83, **182**
Trumeau, 39, <u>40</u>, 119, <u>164</u>
Tubs, 122, **123**, 124
Turbeville, Deborah, 8

Upholstered furniture
    choosing, <u>57</u>
    fabric choices for, 52, 56, 59, 60,
        65, **65**, 66
Urns, **148–49**, 150, **151**

Vanity table, for bathroom, 128, **129**
Vases, 194
Velvet, 65
Venice lace, <u>119</u>
Verbena, <u>153</u>
Versailles, 8, 72
Vinca, <u>153</u>
Vines, 152–53
Vintage decorations and furniture
    beds, 106
    dining room, 93

fireplace surrounds, 40, 42
moldings, 36, 37
size of, 54
table coverings, 97–98

Wallpaper
    borders, as molding, 37
    with glazed or faux finishes,
        48
    murals on, 137
Walls
    adding decorative frame
        molding to, 164–65,
        164
    appliqués on, **35**
    choosing color for, 47–49,
        122
    distressed, 80, 83, **83**
    glazing, 24–25, 48, 49, 83, **83**, 90,
        106, 166–67, **166**
    hand-painting, 106, 168–69, **168,**
        169
    mirrored, 72
    moldings on, 32, **32, 33, 35,**
        36–37, **36**
    panels on, 32, **33, 34–35**, <u>36</u>,
        72, <u>77</u>
    removing, to create open space,
        22, 24, 26
Wave petunias, <u>153</u>
Web sites, vintage moldings from,
    36
Wendy house, <u>159</u>
Window coverings
    atelier, 142
    bathroom, 127
    bedroom, 108
    draperies, 52, 65, 66
Windows
    creating airiness, **26, 27**
    enlarging, 24, 26
    etched glass in, 29, 30, **30**, 83,
        134, **136**
    etching or frosting technique
        for, 172–73, **172, 173**
    as focal point, 62
    frosted, 83
    garden room, 144, **144**
    leaded-glass, **29**, 30
    stained-glass, **29**, 30
    staircase, 134, **136**
    variety of, 30
Wine, decanting, <u>139</u>
Wine cellar, 138, **138**
Wine glasses, **98**
Wisteria, <u>153</u>
Wood, furniture, color of,
    56
Wrought iron, <u>134</u>